Excellence Through Innovation
(Brand Management)

DR. SHYAM BANSHIDHAR SHUKLA

ISBN: 979-8896105121

DEDICATION

Dedicated to my Parents & my students whom I interacted with

directly or indirectly.

TABLE OF CONTENTS

vii

S

ACKNOWLEDGMENTS

I extend my heartfelt gratitude to my students across various

batches since 2005.

Each stream, each group has been a source of constant inspiration,

fueling my passion for teaching and shaping the vision behind this

book.

A special note of thanks to my daughter **Suyesha** and my wife

Seema,

whose unwavering support and encouragement made the

completion of this book possible.

PROLOGUE

In today's fast-paced and highly competitive environment, *Excellence Through Innovation* explores the critical role of **brand management** in achieving sustainable success.

This book delves into how the fusion of **creativity**, **strategic thinking**, and **technological advancement** fuels brand excellence.

Through real-world case studies—ranging from **global giants** to **emerging disruptors**—it uncovers the **key principles** of building, sustaining, and evolving a brand in dynamic markets.

With actionable frameworks and practical insights, readers will discover how to leverage innovation to **enhance brand impact**, **stay ahead of the curve,** and **foster long-term customer loyalty**.

Understanding the Roots of Branding

A **brand** is more than just a name, symbol, or design—it is the unique identity that distinguishes an **institution, product, or service provider**.

Branding can be traced back to ancient civilizations:

- In **2700 BC**, Egyptians branded cattle to prevent theft.

- In **1266**, English bakers were legally required to imprint symbols on their products.

- Many Japanese companies have preserved their brand legacy for over **200 years**.

The 19th century saw branding become more prominent with the rise of **marketing, manufacturing**, and **business management** as professional fields.

Today, branding plays a vital role not only in commercial enterprises but also in the **sustainable growth of educational institutions**, contributing to economic, moral, and ethical development within communities.

Branding as Consumer Perception

According to **Keller (2003)**, a brand exists in the mind of the consumer through the associations and perceptions stored in memory.

These associations help organize information and influence **purchase decisions**.

Biel (1992) emphasized that **brand image** comprises three sub-dimensions:

- **User image**
- **Corporate image**
- **Product/service image**

Further empirical studies, such as those by **Chang, Che, and Chung (2008)**, confirmed the impact of brand image on brand equity, especially in the service sector.

However, these sub-dimensions are often **interdependent** and not considered in isolation.

Branding in a Cultural Context

Meredith Eumont and Dr. Stahl (2010) found that modern branding has evolved beyond traditional advertising.

In an oversaturated marketplace, it is not the product but the **brand** that drives differentiation.

Hofstede's cultural dimensions provide a framework for understanding how brands connect with consumers across cultures.

The five dimensions include:

1. Power Distance

2. Individualism vs. Collectivism

3. Masculinity vs. Femininity

4. Uncertainty Avoidance

5. Long-term vs. Short-term Orientation

Brands that align their messages with cultural values are more likely to **resonate** with target audiences.

For example:

- In high uncertainty avoidance and low power distance cultures, consumers favor **"friendly"** brand personalities.
- In high power distance cultures, **"prestigious"** traits are more appealing.

As **de Mooij** noted, *"When consumer values align with brand values, the effectiveness of advertising increases significantly."*

The Psychological Dimension of Branding

A brand is not just a utility—it carries **symbolic value**.

- **Utilitarian attitudes** are about function and reward.
- **Symbolic attitudes** reflect identity and values.

Branding has the power to shift these perceptions.

For instance:

- A plain soft drink becomes **Coca-Cola**, a symbol of refreshment and heritage.

- Generic shoes become **Nike**, synonymous with aspiration and performance.

- A fast-food item becomes **McDonald's**, representing familiarity and convenience.

As **Jeff Bezos** aptly said, *"A brand is what people say about you when you're not in the room."*

Branding in Higher Education

Dr. Joo-Gim Heaney, **Dr. Peter Ryan**, and **Dr. Michael F. Heaney** highlight the strategic role of branding in **private higher education**, especially in Australia.

These institutions, though often smaller, compete globally and specialize in fields like **business**, **IT**, **hospitality**, and the **creative industries**.

Despite their flexibility and niche focus, branding remains a challenge for smaller institutions, which must position themselves effectively in a **crowded and competitive education market**.

Why Consumers Choose Educational Brands

Whether in business or education, **brands are built to satisfy consumer needs**.

For an educational institution, key brand drivers include:

- **Name recognition**
- **Perceived quality**
- **Price and value**
- **Promotional presence**
- **Packaging** (campus, website, brochures)

- **Emotional and symbolic associations**

To influence choice, an institution's branding must align with the **consumer's personality, motives, and environment**.

1 -A

Services are intangible, but advertising makes them tangible.

ADVERTISING STRATEGIES

Institutional Advertising

Institutional advertising is a strategic approach that focuses on promoting the image, values, and mission of an institution rather than selling specific products or services.

This type of advertising aims to build a positive perception and strong reputation for the institution among its target audiences.

Here are key strategies for effective institutional advertising:

Define Clear Objectives

Establish the goals of the advertising campaign, such as enhancing public perception, attracting talent, increasing stakeholder engagement, or building brand equity.

Clear objectives guide the development and execution of the campaign.

Identify Target Audience

Understand and segment the audience based on demographics, psychographics, and behavior.

This ensures the advertising messages resonate with the intended recipients, whether they are potential students, donors, employees, or the general public.

Craft a Compelling Message

Develop a narrative that highlights the institution's core values, achievements, and unique attributes.

The message should be authentic, memorable, and aligned with the institution's overall branding strategy.

Emphasize elements like history, mission, community impact, and future vision.

Leverage Multiple Channels

Utilize a mix of traditional and digital media to reach a broad audience.

This includes print ads, television and radio spots, social media platforms, content marketing, and institutional websites.

Consistent messaging across all channels reinforces brand identity.

Engage Storytelling

Use storytelling techniques to create emotional connections with the audience.

Share success stories, testimonials, and case studies that illustrate the institution's positive impact and contributions to society.

Emphasize Visual Identity

Incorporate the institution's visual elements, such as logos, colors, and typography, in all advertising materials.

A strong visual identity enhances recognition and reinforces the brand.

Monitor and Adjust

Track the performance of the advertising campaign through metrics such as audience reach, engagement levels, and perception changes.

Use this data to refine strategies and improve future campaigns.

Institutional advertising is a powerful tool for shaping public perception and building a robust institutional brand.

By defining clear objectives, understanding the target audience, crafting compelling messages, leveraging multiple channels, engaging in storytelling, emphasizing visual identity, and continuously monitoring performance, institutions can effectively enhance their reputation and achieve their branding goals.

Alumni Engagement

Alumni engagement is crucial for the sustained growth and reputation of educational institutions.

Effective alumni engagement strategies foster a strong sense of community, loyalty, and support among former students.

Here are several techniques to enhance alumni engagement:

Personalized Communication

Tailor communications to individual alumni based on their interests, achievements, and past interactions with the institution.

Use personalized emails, newsletters, and social media messages to keep them informed and involved.

Social Media Engagement

Create active alumni groups on platforms like LinkedIn, Facebook, and Instagram.

Regularly post updates, success stories, and event invitations.

Encourage alumni to share their experiences and achievements.

Alumni Events

Host reunions, networking events, webinars, and regional meetups.

These events provide opportunities for alumni to reconnect with each other and the institution.

Virtual events can also be effective in reaching a broader audience.

Mentorship Programs

Establish programs where alumni can mentor current students or recent graduates.

This not only benefits the mentees but also allows alumni to give back to the community in a meaningful way.

Career Services and Networking

Offer career development resources, job boards, and professional networking opportunities.

Alumni are more likely to stay engaged if they see tangible benefits in their professional lives.

Volunteer Opportunities

Invite alumni to participate in institutional activities such as admissions interviews, guest lectures, and community service projects.

Volunteering strengthens their connection to the institution.

Recognition and Awards

Acknowledge and celebrate alumni achievements through awards, features in publications, and spotlight stories on the institution's website and social media.

Public recognition fosters pride and loyalty.

Exclusive Content and Benefits

Provide access to exclusive content, such as research reports, online courses, and webinars.

Offer benefits like discounts on events, merchandise, and continuing education programs.

Feedback and Surveys

Regularly solicit feedback from alumni to understand their needs and preferences.

Use surveys to gather insights and improve engagement strategies based on their input.

Alumni Giving Campaigns

Develop targeted fundraising campaigns that highlight specific projects or needs.

Show how alumni contributions directly impact the institution and its current students.

Effective alumni engagement requires a multifaceted approach that combines personalized communication, social media interaction, events, mentorship, career support, volunteer opportunities, recognition, exclusive benefits, feedback mechanisms, and giving campaigns.

By implementing these techniques, institutions can cultivate a loyal and active alumni community that supports and promotes their mission and values.

Audience Analysis

Audience analysis is a critical component of institutional branding, as it helps an institution understand the characteristics, needs, and preferences of its target audiences.

This understanding enables the institution to tailor its branding strategies effectively.

Here are key steps and considerations for conducting an audience analysis for institutional branding:

Identify Audience Segments

- *Prospective Students* – Future students looking for educational opportunities.

- *Current Students* – Individuals currently enrolled in the institution.

- *Alumni* – Graduates who can offer support, donations, and advocacy.

- *Parents and Families* – Influential in the decision-making process for prospective students.

- *Faculty and Staff* – Employees who shape the institution's culture and reputation.

- *Donors and Sponsors* – Financial supporters of the institution.

- *Community Members* – Residents and businesses in the institution's locality.

- *Industry Partners* – Companies and organizations collaborating with the institution.

Demographic Analysis

- *Age* – Identify age groups within each segment to tailor messages accordingly.

- *Gender* – Understand gender distribution to address specific needs and preferences.

- *Location* – Analyze geographic locations to customize regional marketing efforts.

- *Income Level* – Assess economic backgrounds for targeted financial aid and scholarship information.

Psychographic Analysis

- *Values and Beliefs* – Understand what the audience values and believes in.

- *Interests and Hobbies* – Identify common interests to create relevant content and programs.

- *Lifestyle Choices* – Analyze lifestyle patterns to align branding messages with audience behaviors.

Behavioral Analysis

- *Engagement Patterns* – Track how different segments interact with the institution (e.g., event attendance, website visits, social media engagement).

- *Decision-Making Process* – Understand the factors influencing their decisions, such as academic reputation, campus facilities, or career opportunities.

- *Feedback and Reviews* – Collect and analyze feedback from current and past students, parents, and other stakeholders.

Needs and Preferences

- *Educational Needs* – Identify the specific academic and extracurricular interests of prospective and current students.

- *Communication Preferences* – Determine preferred communication channels (e.g., email, social media, direct mail).

- *Support Services* – Understand what services (e.g., career counseling, mental health resources) are most valued.

Competitive Analysis

- *Benchmarking* – Compare audience perceptions and engagement with competitors.

- *Differentiators* – Identify what makes your institution unique from the perspective of your audience.

Data Collection Methods

- *Surveys and Questionnaires* – Gather quantitative and qualitative data directly from audience members.

- *Focus Groups* – Conduct in-depth discussions to gain deeper insights.

- *Social Media Analytics* – Monitor social media interactions to understand audience interests and sentiments.

- *Institutional Data* – Use existing data from enrollment, alumni records, and other internal sources.

Audience analysis is foundational to institutional branding.

By comprehensively understanding the demographic, psychographic, and behavioral characteristics of target audiences, institutions can create effective, tailored branding strategies that resonate with each segment.

This ensures a more focused approach, leading to higher engagement, stronger loyalty, and a better overall reputation for the institution.

Case Study: ABC University

ABC University's Comprehensive Advertising and Marketing Strategy

ABC University, one of the most prestigious educational institutions globally, employs a multifaceted advertising and marketing strategy to maintain its elite status and attract top-tier students. The university's approach combines digital innovation with traditional methods to ensure continued global recognition and enrollment success.

Digital Marketing

Social Media Advertising

Platforms: Facebook, Instagram, Twitter, LinkedIn, YouTube.

Content:

- *Instagram* – Posts featuring student life, campus events, and historical highlights.

- *LinkedIn* – Articles and updates about research breakthroughs, faculty achievements, and alumni success stories.

- *YouTube* – Videos of lectures, campus tours, and student testimonials.

Search Engine Optimization (SEO)

Content: High-quality articles, research papers, and news updates published on the university website.

Keywords: Targeting phrases like "best universities in the world,"

"ABC University research," and program-specific searches such as "ABC MBA."

Pay-Per-Click (PPC) Advertising

Google Ads: Sponsored links for executive education courses and program pages.

Retargeting: Ads aimed at users who have previously visited the ABC University website or engaged with digital content.

Content Marketing

Blogging and Articles

- *University Gazette:* Official news site featuring stories on research, innovation, and campus life.

- *Medium Contributions:* Faculty and students publish articles on topics ranging from public policy to scientific discoveries.

E-books and Guides

- *Admissions Guides:* Detailed breakdowns of the admissions process, financial aid options, and program details.
- *Research Compendiums:* Summaries of key academic research and interdisciplinary breakthroughs.

Video Marketing

YouTube Channel

Content: Lectures, interviews, campus highlights, and testimonials.

Engagement: Live-streamed events such as commencement and guest speaker sessions.

Virtual Tours and 360-Degree Videos

Experience: Interactive online tours providing a comprehensive look at the campus, labs, libraries, and dormitories.

Email Marketing

Newsletters

Content: Monthly updates featuring institutional milestones, alumni achievements, and announcements.

Segmentation: Customized for prospective students, enrolled students, alumni, and donors.

Drip Campaigns

Automation: Series of timed emails guiding prospective students through the admissions process.

Personalization: Emails tailored based on users' interests and online interactions with the university.

Events and Webinars

Open Houses and Information Sessions

- *On-Campus:* For admitted students and families – includes campus tours, panels, and faculty interaction.

- *Virtual:* Webinars covering academic programs, student life, and financial aid.

Workshops and Masterclasses

Content: Sessions led by renowned faculty and guest experts to showcase academic excellence.

Attraction: Featuring influential speakers from academia and industry.

Collaborations and Partnerships

Industry Partnerships

Programs: Research collaborations and internship pipelines with top companies.

Visibility: Publicized partnerships that highlight real-world impact.

School and Community Engagement

Outreach: Engaging with schools and local communities through fairs, workshops, and sponsorships.

Sponsorships: Support for educational events and initiatives.

Traditional Advertising

Print Media

Mediums: Newspapers, academic journals, and educational magazines.

Content: Program highlights, research accolades, and institutional stories.

Outdoor Advertising

Billboards and Transit Ads: Strategically placed in high-traffic cities and international travel hubs.

Alumni Networks and Word of Mouth

Alumni Testimonials

Stories: Features across social media, websites, and brochures.

Events: Alumni reunions and career networking sessions.

Referral Programs

Incentives: Recognition and opportunities for alumni who refer applicants.

Ambassadors: Alumni serving as brand ambassadors and advocates.

ABC University's comprehensive strategy ensures continued brand strength, global visibility, and top-tier student recruitment. By integrating modern digital approaches with trusted traditional methods, the university remains at the forefront of higher education marketing and reinforces its global legacy.

University's comprehensive approach combines digital innovation with traditional methods to maintain its reputation and attract the best students globally. This strategy ensures that the university remains at the forefront of higher education marketing and continues to build its legacy.

2 -B

Brands make people to trust on you and buy your product or services by paying premium.

Brand Ambassadors

Students make impactful brand ambassadors for institutions due to their reliability, authenticity, and reach within their peer networks. By empowering students to advocate for the institution, it fosters a sense of ownership and pride. They can create engaging content, participate in campus events, and share their experiences organically on social media, effectively reaching prospective students and stakeholders. With proper guidance and support, students can authentically represent the institution's values, culture, and offerings, enhancing its reputation and visibility among their peers and beyond.

Managing Brand Ambassadors for institutional branding requires a strategic approach to leverage their influence effectively. Guidelines may be followed as given below :-

Selection: Choose ambassadors whose values align closely with the institution's ethos. Look for individuals with credibility, reach, and a genuine connection to your brand. Whether they're alumni, industry experts, or respected figures, ensure they embody the image you want to project.

Training: Educate ambassadors about your institution's history, mission, and current initiatives. Provide them with key messaging points and equip them to articulate your brand story authentically. Offer media training if necessary to ensure they represent your institution professionally in interviews and public appearances.

Empowerment : Give ambassadors autonomy to express their unique perspectives while advocating for your brand. Encourage them to create content that resonates with their audience while staying aligned with your branding guidelines. Foster a collaborative relationship where they feel valued and supported.

Consistent Communication : Maintain regular communication with ambassadors to keep them updated on institutional developments and campaign objectives. Provide them with relevant resources, such as graphics, press releases, and event invitations. Encourage feedback and address any concerns promptly to nurture a positive partnership.

Recognition and Incentives : Acknowledge the contributions of ambassadors publicly and privately. Highlight their involvement through social media shoutouts, blog features, or awards. Offer incentives such as exclusive access to events, networking opportunities, or branded merchandise to reinforce their commitment.

Performance Evaluation : Monitor the impact of ambassador activities on institutional branding metrics, such as brand awareness, reputation, and engagement. Collect feedback from stakeholders and analyze data to assess the effectiveness of campaigns. Adjust strategies as needed to optimize results and maximize ROI.

Long-term Relationship Building : Cultivate lasting relationships with ambassadors beyond individual campaigns. Invest in their personal and professional development, celebrate their achievements, and stay connected even when they're not actively promoting your brand. Building trust and loyalty fosters a strong network of advocates who champion your institution over time. Brand Ambassadors can elevate the institution's branding efforts and amplify its message to a wider audience.

Brand identity

Managing brand identity involves maintaining consistency in visual elements, messaging, and experiences across all touchpoints. Define brand guidelines to ensure uniformity in logo usage, colors, fonts, and tone of voice. Regularly audit communications to ensure they align with brand values and objectives. Monitor brand sentiment and adapt strategies as needed to maintain relevance and resonance with the target audience. Foster a cohesive brand culture internally to ensure all stakeholders understand and embody the brand identity. By proactively managing brand identity, organizations can build trust, loyalty, and differentiation in the marketplace.

Brand loyalty

Managing an institution's brand loyalty involves fostering a strong emotional connection and sense of belonging among stakeholders. Focus on delivering consistent quality in products, services, and interactions to build trust and satisfaction. Engage with stakeholders regularly through personalized communication, feedback channels, and loyalty programs to demonstrate appreciation and incentivize repeat engagement. Showcase the institution's values, achievements, and impact to reinforce its relevance and inspire pride among stakeholders. Cultivate a positive brand reputation through transparent communication, ethical practices, and social responsibility initiatives. Actively listen to feedback and address concerns promptly to demonstrate commitment to stakeholder satisfaction. By prioritizing stakeholder relationships and consistently delivering value, institutions can cultivate enduring brand loyalty, advocacy, and support, driving long-term success and sustainability.

Case Study: Leveraging Brand Ambassadors for Institutional Branding

Brand ambassadors play a pivotal role in promoting and establishing the brand identity of institutions, be it educational, corporate, or non-profit organizations. This case study explores the strategic use of brand ambassadors in enhancing the brand image and reach of an educational institution.

Institution Overview

XYZ University - is a mid-sized private university known for its strong emphasis on liberal arts education and a commitment to fostering a diverse and inclusive campus environment. Despite its quality education and supportive community, XYZ University faces challenges in attracting a broader pool of applicants and enhancing its visibility in the competitive higher education landscape.

Objectives

1. Increase Visibility: Amplify the university's presence in regional, national, and international markets.

2. Boost Enrollment: Attract a higher number of high-quality applicants.

3. Enhance Reputation: Strengthen the institution's reputation as a premier place for higher education.

Strategy

XYZ University decided to implement a brand ambassador program targeting three main groups: current students, alumni, and faculty. Each group was chosen for their unique ability to resonate with different target audiences.

Implementation

Selection of Brand Ambassadors:

Current Students: Select students who are academically accomplished, actively involved in campus life, and have a strong social media presence.

Alumni: Engage successful alumni who have made significant contributions in their fields and maintain a positive connection with the university.

Faculty: Include renowned faculty members who are thought leaders in their disciplines.

Training and Empowerment:

Provide training sessions on effective communication, social media usage, and the university's brand values.

Develop a toolkit containing marketing materials, brand guidelines, and messaging templates.

Activities and Campaigns:

Social Media Campaigns: Ambassadors share their experiences and achievements using dedicated hashtags and participate in Q&A sessions with prospective students.

Campus Tours and Open Days: Ambassadors lead virtual and in-person tours, sharing personal anecdotes and highlighting unique aspects of the university.

Content Creation: Ambassadors contribute to blog posts, video testimonials, and podcasts, providing authentic and relatable content.

Community Engagement: Participate in local and international events, representing the university and engaging with potential students and their families.

Incentives and Recognition:

Offer incentives such as scholarships, exclusive networking

opportunities, and recognition at university events.

Create an annual awards program to honor the most impactful ambassadors.

Outcomes

Increased Visibility:

The social media campaigns led to a 35% increase in followers and engagement on the university's platforms.

The content created by brand ambassadors reached over 500,000 potential students globally.

Boosted Enrollment:

Applications increased by 20% in the following admission cycle.

There was a notable rise in the diversity of applicants, with more international and out-of-state students showing interest.

Enhanced Reputation:

The university received positive media coverage and was featured in several educational magazines and online portals.

Alumni and faculty involvement bolstered the institution's credibility and prestige.

The brand ambassador program at XYZ University successfully enhanced the institution's visibility, boosted enrollment, and strengthened its reputation. By leveraging the authentic voices of current students, alumni, and faculty, the university was able to create a powerful and relatable brand narrative. This case demonstrates the effectiveness of a well-structured brand ambassador program in achieving institutional branding objectives.

Q. Design similar program for Institution of our choice.

52

Brand strategy

An institution's brand strategy is crucial for establishing its identity, credibility, and competitive edge. A robust brand strategy begins with a clear understanding of the institution's mission, vision, and values, ensuring these elements resonate with its target audience. Key components include defining a unique value proposition that distinguishes the institution from competitors, focusing on the specific benefits and unique experiences it offers.

Effective brand positioning is central, aiming to occupy a distinct place in the minds of stakeholders, including students, faculty, alumni, and partners. This involves consistent messaging across all touch points, ensuring that the brand voice, tone, and visual identity align with the institution's core values and goals.

A successful brand strategy leverages storytelling to create emotional connections, sharing impactful narratives that highlight the institution's achievements, culture, and community. This can be achieved through various channels, including social media, digital marketing, public relations, and events.

Engagement and feedback mechanisms are vital, allowing the institution to understand perceptions and adjust its strategies accordingly. Continuous monitoring and evaluation help maintain brand relevance and adapt to changing trends and audience needs.

An institution's brand strategy should be comprehensive and dynamic, focusing on differentiation, consistency, and engagement. It should create a compelling narrative that not only

attracts but also retains and nurtures relationships with its

audience, ultimately fostering loyalty and advocacy.

3-C

A powerful brand connects with emotions, as emotions are the driving force behind most, if not all, of our decisions.

Communication channels

Institutional communication channels are essential for effectively disseminating information and engaging with diverse stakeholders, including students, faculty, staff, alumni, and the broader community. These channels ensure the institution's messages are consistently and coherently delivered, reinforcing its brand identity and strategic objectives.

Key communication channels include:

Digital Platforms : Websites and social media platforms (such as Facebook, Twitter, LinkedIn, Instagram, and YouTube) are pivotal for reaching a wide audience quickly. They provide updates, promote events, share achievements, and engage in real-time interactions.

Email Newsletters : Regularly scheduled newsletters keep stakeholders informed about news, events, and important updates. They are an effective way to maintain direct and personalized communication.

Intranet Systems : For internal communication, intranets provide a centralized platform for faculty and staff to access resources, share information, and collaborate on projects.

Mobile Apps : Custom apps enhance accessibility, offering on-the-go access to institutional news, resources, and services, improving engagement with tech-savvy audiences.

Print Media Despite the digital shift, print media such as brochures, magazines, and annual reports remain valuable for detailed content and formal communication.

Public Relations and Media Outreach : Press releases, media kits, and relationships with journalists help in amplifying the institution's voice and managing its public image.

Events and Webinars : These platforms facilitate direct interaction, offering opportunities for engagement, feedback, and community building.

Bulletin Boards and Digital Signage : On-campus visual communication tools ensure important messages reach students and staff physically present in the institution.

Effective use of these channels requires a strategic approach, ensuring that each channel complements the others, maintains consistent messaging, and effectively reaches its intended audience. This multi-channel strategy helps in fostering a connected and informed institutional community.

Community relations

Community relations involve building and maintaining positive relationships between an institution and its surrounding community. Effective community relations foster goodwill, mutual support, and collaboration. This includes engaging in local events, supporting community initiatives, offering educational and cultural programs, and maintaining open communication channels. By actively participating in and contributing to the community, the institution enhances its reputation, strengthens ties with local stakeholders, and creates a supportive environment that benefits both the community and the institution. Strong community relations also encourage local support, attract prospective students, and promote a sense of belonging and shared purpose.

Competitive analysis

A competitive analysis of an institution's branding involves evaluating its brand positioning, messaging, and identity against its key competitors. This process identifies strengths, weaknesses, opportunities, and threats in the branding landscape.

Brand Positioning : Assess where the institution stands in the market relative to competitors. Determine its unique value proposition and how it differentiates itself through programs, faculty expertise, campus facilities, and student outcomes.

Messaging and Tone : Analyze the clarity and consistency of messaging. Effective branding communicates a clear mission, vision, and values that resonate with target audiences. Compare how competitors articulate their brand stories and core messages.

Visual Identity : Examine the institution's visual elements such as logos, color schemes, typography, and overall design aesthetics. A strong visual identity should be distinctive and memorable, creating a cohesive look across all platforms. Compare with competitors to see how well the brand stands out.

Digital Presence : Review the institution's online presence, including its website, social media, and digital marketing efforts.

Effective digital branding engages audiences, provides valuable content, and fosters community interaction. Evaluate the user experience and engagement levels compared to competitors.

Alumni and Community Engagement : Assess how the institution involves alumni and the broader community in its branding efforts. Strong alumni networks and active community engagement can significantly enhance brand reputation.

By systematically comparing these elements, the institution can identify areas for improvement, leverage its strengths, and better position itself in the competitive educational landscape.

Consistency in branding

Consistency in branding is vital for establishing a strong, recognizable identity that resonates with audiences and builds trust. It ensures that all brand elements, including messaging, visual identity, and tone, are uniform across all touchpoints. This uniformity reinforces the brand's core values and mission, making it easily identifiable and memorable.

Consistent branding involves using the same logos, color schemes, typography, and voice in all communications, from marketing materials and social media to internal documents and customer interactions. This coherence helps prevent confusion, reinforces brand promises, and creates a seamless experience for stakeholders.

Moreover, consistency builds credibility and professionalism, which are crucial for long-term brand loyalty. It also facilitates better recognition and recall, making it easier for the audience to associate positive experiences with the brand. Ultimately, a consistent branding strategy enhances the overall perception and value of the institution, fostering trust and engagement.

Case

XYZ University embarked on a comprehensive branding strategy to boost its global visibility, attract diverse talent, strengthen alumni relationships, and promote academic excellence. By revamping its website for better user experience, leveraging social media for engagement, and using content marketing, XYZU effectively showcased its achievements and campus life. Traditional media efforts included press releases, media coverage, and print materials, while events like open days, campus tours, and virtual webinars targeted prospective students. Collaborations with influencers expanded reach, and alumni stories and networking events fostered a strong community. Academic publications and conferences highlighted faculty research, enhancing XYZU 's reputation. These multi-channel efforts led to a 25% increase in applications, improved global rankings, stronger alumni engagement, and more international research collaborations, successfully positioning XYZU as a leading institution globally.

65

4 -D

Branding isn't just about standing out as better than your competitors; it's about being perceived as the only solution to your audience's problem.

Digital Branding

Digital branding for an institution involves creating a strong online presence that reflects its values, mission, and strengths. It encompasses a cohesive strategy across various digital platforms, including a well-designed website, active social media profiles, and engaging content marketing. Key elements include a distinctive visual identity, such as a logo and color scheme, consistent messaging, and a user-friendly digital experience. SEO and online advertising enhance visibility, while data analytics inform strategy adjustments. Engaging storytelling and showcasing achievements build trust and reputation. Effective digital branding attracts prospective students, staff, and partners, and fosters a loyal community by consistently delivering value and maintaining a positive, recognizable presence in the digital space.

Differentiation in Institutional Branding

To **stand out in a competitive educational landscape,** institutions must establish distinctive qualities. Differentiation strategies include:

1. Unique Programs and Curriculum

Offering specialized, niche courses that aren't widely available can attract students with focused interests.

2. Innovative Teaching Methods

Adopting forward-thinking methods like **flipped classrooms, experiential learning,** and **technology integration** enriches the learning experience.

3. Exceptional Faculty

Hiring and retaining top-tier educators and researchers boosts credibility and attracts talent.

4. Strong Industry Partnerships

Collaborations with industry for **internships, research**, and **placements** enhance student employability.

5. State-of-the-Art Facilities

Investments in advanced labs, libraries, and recreational amenities elevate campus life.

6. Global Opportunities

Programs like **study abroad, student exchanges**, and **international collaborations** appeal to globally minded students.

7. Emphasis on Research and Innovation

Prioritizing research creates opportunities for breakthroughs and draws top academics.

8. Community Engagement

Local outreach and service projects strengthen institutional impact and reputation.

9. Personalized Education

Providing tailored support through **advising, mentorship**, and **career guidance** supports student success.

10. Sustainability and Social Responsibility

Leading in **green practices** and **social impact initiatives** resonates with socially conscious students.

Combining these elements allows institutions to build a unique brand identity that attracts attention and fosters long-term growth.

Case Study: Communication Channels for Institutional Branding

Background

A leading university, Evergreen State University (ESU), decided to enhance its brand image and attract a global audience of students, faculty, and partners. To achieve this, ESU implemented a comprehensive branding strategy that utilized multiple communication channels.

Objectives

1. Increase global visibility and brand recognition.

2. Attract a diverse and talented pool of students and faculty.

3. Strengthen relationships with alumni and partners.

4. Promote academic and research excellence.

Strategy and Implementation

Digital and Social Media

Website: ESU revamped its website to be more user-friendly, visually appealing, and mobile-responsive. The new site featured detailed information about academic programs, campus life, research initiatives, and success stories.

Social Media Platforms: The university leveraged platforms like Facebook, Twitter, Instagram, LinkedIn, and YouTube to share updates, engage with the community, and showcase achievements. Regular posts included student testimonials, faculty research highlights, event promotions, and alumni success stories.

Content Marketing: ESU started a blog featuring articles written by faculty, students, and alumni. Topics ranged from academic advice and research insights to personal experiences and career guidance.

Traditional Media

Press Releases and Media Coverage: The university maintained relationships with local, national, and international media outlets to ensure coverage of major events, breakthroughs in research, and notable achievements.

Print Materials: Brochures, flyers, and posters were designed and distributed at educational fairs, partner institutions, and through mail campaigns targeting potential students and donors.

Events and Partnerships

Open Days and Campus Tours: Regularly scheduled events allowed prospective students and their families to visit the campus, interact with faculty and current students, and get a feel for university life.

Webinars and Online Workshops: For international audiences, ESU hosted webinars and virtual tours, providing an interactive platform to learn about the university's offerings and culture.

Collaborations with Influencers: The university partnered with educational influencers and bloggers to reach wider audiences through authentic testimonials and reviews.

Alumni Network

Alumni Stories: Successful alumni were featured in campaigns across various channels to highlight the long-term value and impact of an ESU education.

Networking Events: Exclusive alumni events facilitated networking and mentorship opportunities, strengthening the sense of community and loyalty.

Donor Campaigns: Targeted campaigns were designed to engage alumni in giving back, emphasizing the importance of their contributions to future generations.

Academic and Research Publications

Journals and Publications: Faculty research was regularly published in esteemed journals, and the university's own academic publications were widely distributed.

Conferences and Seminars: Hosting and participating in national and international conferences enhanced the university's reputation as a leader in research and innovation.

Outcomes

Increased Enrollments: There was a 25% increase in applications from both domestic and international students within two years.

Enhanced Reputation: The university saw a significant rise in global rankings and was featured more frequently in academic and mainstream media.

Stronger Community Engagement: Alumni engagement increased by 40%, with more alumni participating in events and contributing to fundraising efforts.

Greater Research Collaboration: The number of international research collaborations and grants increased, enhancing the university's academic stature.

The multi-channel communication strategy adopted by Evergreen State University proved to be highly effective in enhancing its brand image and achieving its strategic objectives. By leveraging both digital and traditional media, fostering community relationships, and showcasing academic excellence, ESU successfully positioned itself as a leading institution on the global stage.

5-E

Strong brands don't pursue customers; they attract them by remaining authentic to their identity.

Educational Institutions Branding

Engagement metrics

Events branding

Branding for educational institutions is crucial for establishing a strong identity, attracting prospective students, and maintaining a positive reputation. Here are key components:

Clear Mission and Vision : Articulate the institution's purpose and long-term goals. This helps stakeholders understand the institution's values and aspirations.

Distinct Visual Identity : Develop a recognizable logo, color scheme, and typography. Consistent visual elements across all materials reinforce brand recognition.

Compelling Storytelling : Share stories of student achievements, faculty expertise, and institutional milestones. Highlighting success stories can inspire and attract prospective students.

Quality Content Marketing : Produce high-quality content, such as blog posts, videos, and social media updates, to engage with the audience and provide value. Educational articles, campus news, and event highlights keep the audience informed and interested.

Responsive Website : Ensure the institution's website is user-friendly, mobile-optimized, and visually appealing. It should provide easy access to information about programs, admissions, campus life, and contact details.

Social Media Presence : Maintain active profiles on popular social media platforms. Engage with followers through regular updates, live events, and interactive content.

SEO and Online Advertising : Use search engine optimization to improve the institution's online visibility. Online advertising campaigns can target specific demographics and drive traffic to the institution's website.

Alumni Network : Leverage the success of alumni to build credibility and attract new students. Alumni testimonials and success stories can be powerful endorsements.

Community Engagement : Participate in and sponsor community events. Building strong relationships with local communities enhances the institution's reputation and demonstrates social responsibility.

Consistent Messaging : Ensure all communications, from promotional materials to social media posts, reflect the institution's core values and messaging. Consistency builds trust and reinforces the brand identity.

By focusing on these elements, educational institutions can create a strong, recognizable brand that resonates with students, faculty, alumni, and the wider community.

Engagement Metrics

Engagement metrics are crucial indicators of how effectively an institution connects with its audience. Key metrics include:

Website Traffic : Measures the number of visitors and page

views. High traffic indicates strong interest and visibility.

Bounce Rate : The percentage of visitors who leave the site after viewing only one page. A low bounce rate suggests engaging content.

Time on Site : The average duration visitors spend on the site. Longer times indicate compelling content and user interest.

Social Media Metrics   Includes likes, shares, comments, and followers. These metrics gauge audience interaction and content resonance.

Email Open and Click-Through Rates : Measure the effectiveness of email campaigns. High rates indicate that the audience finds the emails valuable.

Conversion Rates : The percentage of visitors who take a desired action, such as filling out a form or applying. High conversion rates reflect successful engagement strategies.

Event Attendance : Tracks participation in both virtual and in-person events, indicating audience interest and engagement.

These metrics provide valuable insights into the effectiveness of an institution's engagement efforts and inform strategic adjustments.

Events branding

Branding for events involves creating a distinctive and memorable identity that attracts attendees and promotes engagement. Here are key elements to consider:

Clear Theme and Messaging : Define a cohesive theme that aligns with the event's purpose and audience. Ensure messaging is consistent across all platforms, highlighting key benefits and unique aspects.

Visual Identity : Develop a unique logo, color scheme, and design elements that reflect the event's theme. Use these consistently across promotional materials, social media, and the event website to build recognition.

Engaging Content : Create compelling content to generate excitement. This includes teaser videos, behind-the-scenes looks, speaker spotlights, and informative blog posts. Use storytelling to convey the event's value and relevance.

Social Media Campaigns : Leverage social media platforms to reach a broader audience. Use event-specific hashtags, interactive posts, live updates, and countdowns to build anticipation and engagement.

Influencer Partnerships : Collaborate with influencers or industry leaders to amplify the event's reach. Their endorsements can attract their followers and lend credibility.

Email Marketing : Send targeted email campaigns to potential attendees. Provide valuable information, exclusive offers, and reminders to encourage registration and participation.

User Experience : Ensure a seamless and enjoyable experience, from easy registration processes to engaging on-site activities. Positive experiences enhance brand perception and encourage repeat attendance.

Post-Event Engagement : Continue engaging with attendees after the event through follow-up emails, surveys, and social media interactions. Share event highlights and gather feedback to improve future events.

By focusing on these elements, event branding can create a lasting impression, foster strong connections, and drive successful outcomes.

6 -F

"Your brand is where your self-perception and others' perception meet."

Faculty Involvement

Fundraising Campaigns

Faculty involvement is crucial for branding educational institutions, as they embody academic excellence and innovation. Their active participation can significantly enhance the institution's reputation and appeal. Here are key ways faculty contribute to branding efforts:

Thought Leadership : Faculty enhance the institution's brand by publishing research, presenting at conferences, and writing articles or blog posts. Their expertise positions the institution as a leader in various fields.

Media Engagement : Faculty participation in interviews, podcasts, and webinars broadens the institution's reach. Sharing their knowledge on diverse platforms increases visibility and showcases the institution's strengths.

Social Media Presence : Encouraging faculty to be active on social media humanizes the institution and engages a wider audience. They can share their work, comment on industry trends, and interact with students and peers.

Guest Lectures and Workshops : Faculty represent the institution by giving guest lectures and conducting workshops at other institutions or industry events. This extends the institution's reach and highlights its academic strengths.

Alumni Engagement : Faculty maintain connections with alumni, inviting them to speak at events or contribute to newsletters. Alumni success stories, facilitated by faculty relationships, enhance the institution's reputation.

Student Interaction : Approachable and engaged faculty create a positive learning environment. Student testimonials about supportive and inspiring faculty are powerful marketing tools.

Research and Innovation : Highlighting faculty-led research and innovations attracts prospective students and partners. Showcasing groundbreaking work demonstrates the institution's commitment to advancing knowledge and solving real-world problems.

Community Involvement : Faculty participation in community service and local projects reinforces the institution's commitment to social responsibility and strengthens community ties.

Leveraging faculty expertise and engagement builds a strong, authentic brand that resonates with prospective students, parents, and the academic community, attracting new students and fostering pride and loyalty among all stakeholders.

Fundraising campaigns

Fundraising campaigns for institution branding involve strategic initiatives to engage donors and highlight the institution's mission and impact. Key elements include:

Storytelling : Share compelling narratives about the institution's successes and future goals.

Alumni Engagement : Mobilize alumni through events and personalized outreach.

Social Media : Leverage platforms for wider reach and real-time updates.

Events : Host gala dinners, auctions, and community events to foster donor relationships.

Transparency : Showcase how donations are utilized through detailed reports and testimonials.

These strategies not only raise funds but also enhance the institution's brand by demonstrating its value and impact on the community.

7-G

Your personal brand is a commitment to your clients—a pledge of quality, consistency, expertise, and dependability.

Governance- role in branding

Governance plays a critical role in institutional branding, influencing the perception and reputation of educational institutions. Effective governance ensures transparency, accountability, and strategic direction, all of which contribute to a strong and positive brand. Here's a detailed exploration of how governance impacts institutional branding:

Strategic Vision and Leadership

Vision and Mission Articulation

Governance bodies, such as boards of trustees or regents, are responsible for defining and articulating the institution's vision and mission. This clear sense of purpose guides all branding efforts and ensures that the institution's core values are consistently communicated.

A well-defined vision inspires confidence and attracts students, faculty, donors, and partners who share the institution's goals and values.

Strategic Planning :

Effective governance involves strategic planning, setting long-term goals, and allocating resources efficiently. This planning aligns with branding initiatives, ensuring that marketing efforts support the institution's broader objectives.

Strategic plans often include initiatives to enhance academic programs, research capabilities, and campus facilities, all of which bolster the institution's brand.

Transparency and Accountability

Transparent Decision-Making :

Governance bodies must ensure that decision-making processes are transparent and inclusive. Transparency builds trust among stakeholders, including students, parents, faculty, and the community, reinforcing a positive brand image.

Regularly published reports and open meetings can demonstrate accountability and integrity, which are key components of a reputable brand.

Financial Oversight:

Sound financial management by the governance board is essential for sustainability and growth. Financial stability reflects positively on the institution's brand, suggesting reliability and foresight.

Transparent financial practices and responsible budgeting ensure that resources are used effectively, enhancing the institution's ability to invest in quality education and facilities.

Academic Excellence and Innovation

Quality Assurance :

Governance bodies are responsible for ensuring high academic standards. By overseeing curriculum development, faculty hiring, and research initiatives, they directly impact the quality of education provided.

A commitment to academic excellence and continuous improvement strengthens the institution's brand as a leader in education.

Innovation and Adaptation :

Effective governance encourages innovation in teaching, research, and administration. Institutions that embrace new technologies and methodologies are perceived as forward-thinking and adaptable, enhancing their brand appeal.

Governance support for cutting-edge research and partnerships with industry can position the institution at the forefront of academic and professional advancements.

Community and Stakeholder Engagement

Alumni Relations:

Governance plays a role in fostering strong alumni networks. Engaged alumni are valuable brand ambassadors who can support fundraising efforts, mentor students, and enhance the institution's reputation through their achievements.

Effective governance ensures that alumni relations are maintained and that alumni are regularly involved in institutional activities and decision-making processes.

Community Involvement :

Institutions that are actively involved in their local and global communities build a positive brand image. Governance bodies can spearhead community outreach programs, partnerships, and social responsibility initiatives.

Community engagement demonstrates the institution's commitment to societal impact, which is a compelling aspect of its brand.

Ethical Standards and Social Responsibility

Ethical Governance :

Adhering to high ethical standards in governance practices reinforces the institution's integrity. Policies that promote equity, diversity, and inclusion are essential for building a respectful and inclusive community.

Ethical governance practices help avoid scandals and controversies, which can damage the institution's reputation and brand.

Sustainability Initiatives :

Governance bodies can prioritize sustainability, implementing eco-friendly policies and practices. An institution known for its commitment to sustainability appeals to environmentally conscious students and stakeholders.

Sustainable practices also reflect long-term thinking and responsibility, enhancing the institution's brand as a leader in ethical and responsible education.

Crisis Management and Communication

Effective Crisis Management:

Governance plays a crucial role in crisis management. How an institution responds to crises—be it financial, reputational, or operational—affects its brand significantly.

Having a robust crisis management plan in place, with clear communication strategies, ensures that the institution can navigate challenges while maintaining trust and confidence among stakeholders.

Clear Communication :

Governance bodies must ensure consistent and clear communication across all platforms. This involves not only crisis communication but also regular updates about institutional achievements, changes, and strategic directions.

- Clear, consistent communication helps manage stakeholder expectations and keeps the community informed and engaged, which is vital for a strong brand.

Governance is integral to institutional branding, as it shapes the strategic vision, ensures accountability and transparency, promotes academic excellence, engages with stakeholders, and upholds ethical standards. Effective governance practices foster trust, inspire confidence, and build a robust and positive brand image. By prioritizing sound governance, educational institutions can enhance their reputation, attract top talent, and secure long-term success.

8

Strong brands improve people's lives by simplifying decisions,

fostering trust, and cultivating loyalty.

Human Persona in Brand manifestation

In brand manifestation, the human persona encapsulates a

brand's unique identity, reflecting its personality traits, values,

and beliefs. This concept acknowledges that brands are more than

just products or services; they embody human-like characteristics

that resonate with consumers on an emotional level. Here's a

thorough exploration of the human persona in brand

manifestation:

Defining Personality Traits and Identity

Authenticity : Genuine and consistent actions and messaging build trust and credibility, fostering brand loyalty.

Empathy : Understanding and relating to customers' needs and challenges deepen emotional connections.

Innovation : Forward-thinking and creative brands inspire customers with their vision for the future.

Humor : Brands incorporating humor create positive associations and stand out in the market.

Sincerity: Honest and transparent communication earns respect and admiration from consumers.

Embodying Values and Beliefs

Ethical Responsibility : Brands demonstrate integrity and social consciousness, advocating for positive change.

Diversity and Inclusion : Celebrating differences and promoting equality fosters a sense of belonging for all.

Environmental Stewardship : Commitment to sustainability minimizes ecological footprints and supports conservation efforts.

-Community Engagement : Active involvement in communities

strengthens connections with stakeholders.

Exploring Brand Archetypes

Hero : Brands inspire customers to overcome challenges and achieve their goals.

Everyman/Everywoman : Relatable and authentic brands connect with customers on a personal level.

Sage : Brands educate and empower customers, offering insights and guidance.

Jester : Brands entertain and delight customers, injecting fun into their lives.

Lover : Brands evoke strong emotions and desires, creating deep connections with customers.

Crafting Brand Storytelling and Narrative

Origin Story : Compelling origin stories captivate customers, drawing them into the brand's narrative.

Character Development : Characters or personas embody the brand's values and traits, serving as brand ambassadors.

Emotional Resonance : Brands evoke emotions that deepen customer connection and loyalty.

Consistent Messaging : Coherent storytelling across all touchpoints strengthens brand identity.

Delivering Brand Experience and Interaction

Customer Engagement : Brands engage customers through various channels, building relationships and loyalty.

User Experience : Brands design products and interfaces that reflect their persona, enhancing customer satisfaction.

Brand Voice and Tone : Communication should align with the brand's personality, resonating with its audience.

The human persona in brand manifestation encompasses a range of attributes and values that define a brand's identity and shape its interactions with customers. By embodying authenticity, empathy, and innovation, brands can forge deeper emotional connections and create memorable experiences for their audience.

An example can be XYZ University, embodying characteristics such as prestige, excellence, and tradition. Through its messaging, imagery, and interactions, XYZ cultivates an aura of academic brilliance and intellectual pursuit. Its brand persona resonates with ambitious students, accomplished faculty, and alumni who aspire to make a meaningful impact. XYZ's commitment to innovation and global engagement further enhances its human-like persona, positioning it as a beacon of knowledge and leadership in higher education.

Your brand is a story that unfolds at every point where customers interact with it.

Institutional History - Leveraging

Internal Branding

Institutional history - leveraging

Leveraging institutional history for branding is a powerful strategy for establishing credibility, building a sense of heritage, and fostering pride among stakeholders. By highlighting key milestones, influential figures, and defining moments, institutions can create a compelling narrative that reinforces their identity and values. Here's a comprehensive exploration of how institutional history can be leveraged for branding:

Establishing Credibility and Authority

Institutional history serves as a testament to the institution's longevity and enduring legacy. By tracing its origins back to its founding, institutions can showcase a rich heritage of academic excellence, research contributions, and societal impact. Highlighting notable achievements, such as groundbreaking discoveries, influential alumni, or significant cultural contributions, reinforces the institution's authority in its field and establishes credibility among peers, prospective students, and stakeholders.

Building a Sense of Heritage and Tradition

Institutional history provides a foundation for building a sense of heritage and tradition. By celebrating time-honored customs, rituals, and ceremonies, institutions can create a shared cultural identity that resonates with current students, alumni, and faculty. Embracing traditions fosters a sense of belonging and pride, creating strong emotional connections with the institution and its values. Whether it's commemorating founding anniversaries, honoring past achievements, or preserving historic landmarks, institutions can cultivate a sense of continuity and belonging that strengthens their brand identity.

Showcasing Evolution and Adaptation

Institutional history also reflects the institution's ability to evolve and adapt to changing times. By highlighting pivotal moments of transformation, such as strategic expansions, curriculum innovations, or technological advancements, institutions demonstrate their resilience and relevance in an ever-changing world. Emphasizing a spirit of innovation and progress underscores the institution's forward-thinking approach and its commitment to preparing students for the challenges of the future. By showcasing how the institution has evolved while staying true to its core values, institutions can inspire confidence in their brand and attract forward-looking stakeholders.

Honoring Founders and Visionaries

Institutional history provides an opportunity to honor the visionaries and leaders who have shaped the institution's identity and values. By paying tribute to founding figures, influential presidents, or pioneering faculty members, institutions can reinforce their commitment to excellence and innovation. Sharing stories of leadership, courage, and perseverance not only celebrates the contributions of past leaders but also inspires current and future generations to uphold the institution's legacy and pursue their own ambitions. Recognizing the contributions of trailblazers and visionaries adds depth and authenticity to the institution's brand narrative, fostering a sense of pride and admiration among stakeholders.

Engaging Alumni and Building a Community

Institutional history serves as a bridge between the past, present, and future, connecting alumni with their alma mater and fostering a sense of community. By engaging alumni through reunions, homecoming events, and alumni networks, institutions can tap into a valuable source of support, mentorship, and philanthropy. Sharing stories of alumni achievements, career paths, and personal successes not only celebrates their accomplishments but also strengthens the institution's brand by showcasing the impact of its education and values. By fostering a strong sense of alumni pride and loyalty, institutions can amplify their brand reach and influence, creating a virtuous cycle of engagement and support.

Differentiating the Institution in a Competitive Landscape :

Institutional history provides a unique opportunity to differentiate the institution in a competitive higher education landscape. By showcasing distinctive features, such as unique founding principles, pioneering research endeavors, or notable alumni achievements, institutions can carve out a niche that sets them apart from their peers. Emphasizing what makes the institution unique and special helps attract students, faculty, and partners who resonate with its values and aspirations. By leveraging its rich history as a strategic asset, institutions can position themselves as leaders in their field and create a lasting impact on the communities they serve.

Institutional history is a powerful tool for branding, offering a rich tapestry of stories, achievements, and values that shape the institution's identity and legacy. By leveraging its history to establish credibility, build heritage and tradition, showcase evolution and adaptation, honor founders and visionaries, engage alumni, and differentiate itself in a competitive landscape, an institution can create a compelling brand narrative that resonates with stakeholders and inspires pride and loyalty. Through strategic storytelling and engagement initiatives, institutions can harness the power of their history to strengthen their brand and secure a bright future for generations to come.

Internal branding

Internal branding is the process of aligning and engaging employees with the organization's brand identity, values, and objectives. It focuses on ensuring that employees understand, embrace, and actively promote the brand internally, which ultimately enhances the organization's external reputation and customer experience. Here's a detailed exploration of internal branding:

Brand Alignment

Internal branding begins with ensuring that employees understand and align with the organization's brand identity, mission, and values. This involves communicating the brand's purpose, personality, and promise in a clear and compelling manner. When employees understand what the brand stands for and how they contribute to its success, they are more likely to embody its values and deliver consistent brand experiences to customers.

Employee Engagement

Engaged employees are essential for effective internal branding. Organizations can foster employee engagement by involving them in decision-making processes, providing opportunities for professional development and growth, and recognizing and rewarding their contributions. Engaged employees are more motivated, productive, and committed to delivering exceptional service, which positively impacts the customer experience and strengthens the brand.

Training and Development

Training and development initiatives play a crucial role in internal branding by equipping employees with the knowledge, skills, and resources they need to deliver on the brand promise. This may include brand training sessions, workshops on customer service and communication skills, and ongoing learning opportunities to stay updated on industry trends and best practices. Investing in employee development not only enhances their capabilities but also reinforces their connection to the brand and its values.

Internal Communication

Effective internal communication is essential for fostering a shared understanding of the brand and promoting alignment across the organization. Organizations can use various channels, such as intranet portals, email newsletters, team meetings, and town hall sessions, to communicate the brand's vision, goals, and performance metrics. Transparent and consistent communication builds trust, boosts morale, and empowers employees to act as brand ambassadors both internally and externally.

Leadership and Role Modeling

Leadership plays a critical role in shaping organizational culture and reinforcing the brand values. Leaders should exemplify the desired behaviors and attitudes outlined in the brand identity, serving as role models for employees to emulate. By demonstrating a commitment to the brand and its principles, leaders inspire trust and confidence among employees, driving engagement and fostering a culture of accountability and excellence.

Recognition and Rewards

Recognizing and rewarding employees who exemplify the brand values and deliver exceptional customer experiences reinforces the importance of internal branding. This can take the form of formal recognition programs, peer-to-peer recognition initiatives, or performance-based incentives tied to brand-related metrics. Celebrating success and acknowledging employee contributions not only motivates individuals but also reinforces the organization's commitment to its brand promise.

Feedback and Continuous Improvement

Encouraging feedback from employees and incorporating their input into decision-making processes is essential for continuous improvement and maintaining alignment with the brand. Organizations can gather feedback through surveys, focus groups, and one-on-one conversations to assess employee perceptions of the brand, identify areas for improvement, and implement changes as needed. Engaging employees in the feedback loop demonstrates that their opinions are valued and fosters a culture of collaboration and innovation.

Integration with HR Processes

Internal branding should be integrated into various human resources processes, including recruitment, onboarding, performance management, and succession planning. This ensures that the organization hires, develops, and retains employees who embody the brand values and contribute to its success. HR policies and practices should reflect the organization's commitment to internal branding, reinforcing the importance of aligning employee behaviors with the brand identity.

Internal branding is a holistic approach to aligning employees with the organization's brand identity, values, and objectives. By fostering brand alignment, engaging employees, providing training and development opportunities, promoting effective communication, demonstrating leadership commitment, recognizing and rewarding contributions, soliciting feedback, and

integrating internal branding into HR processes, organizations can

create a culture that supports and reinforces the brand, ultimately

driving employee engagement, customer satisfaction, and

business success. The Intersection of Sustainability and Innovation

10-J

Products are manufactured in factories, but brands are built in the mind.

Judgments of Brand

Judgments of a brand are reflections of consumers' perceptions, shaped by various factors including experiences, beliefs, and associations with the brand. These assessments significantly influence consumer behavior, ultimately determining the brand's success and longevity in the market. Below is a comprehensive exploration of the judgments associated with a brand:

Brand Perception

Brand perception denotes the overall impression or mental picture consumers hold of a brand. It encompasses attributes such as quality, reliability, trustworthiness, and prestige. Consumers form opinions about a brand's image through personal encounters with the brand and information from advertising, word-of-mouth, and other sources. A positive brand perception can lead to favorable assessments, increased loyalty, and a willingness to pay a premium for the brand's offerings.

Perceived Quality

Perceived quality reflects consumers' evaluations regarding the superiority or excellence of a brand's products or services in comparison to those of competitors. Assessments of quality are based on factors such as durability, performance, design, and features. Brands consistently delivering high-quality offerings earn positive judgments, fostering trust and loyalty among consumers. Conversely, brands failing to meet expectations or experiencing quality-related issues may face negative assessments that harm their reputation and diminish consumer trust.

Brand Trust

Brand trust signifies consumers' confidence in the reliability, integrity, and credibility of a brand. Trust is cultivated over time through consistent, dependable interactions with the brand, coupled with transparent communication and ethical business practices. Brands prioritizing customer satisfaction, honoring commitments, and demonstrating accountability gain the trust of consumers, resulting in favorable judgments and enduring relationships. Conversely, brands violating consumer trust through deceptive practices or ethical breaches risk severe criticism and loss of credibility.

Brand Loyalty

Brand loyalty gauges the extent to which consumers consistently choose a particular brand over others and display a willingness to make repeat purchases or advocate for the brand. Loyalty stems from favorable judgments about the brand's value proposition, product performance, and overall customer experience. Brands fostering strong emotional connections, delivering superior offerings, and providing exceptional service are more likely to inspire loyalty. Loyal customers not only drive repeat business but also serve as brand advocates, influencing others' perceptions and bolstering brand growth.

Brand Equity

Brand equity embodies the intangible value or goodwill associated with a brand, encompassing elements such as brand awareness, perceived quality, brand associations, and brand loyalty. Positive judgments of a brand contribute to its brand equity by enhancing consumer preferences, willingness to pay a premium, and advocacy. Brand equity serves as a valuable asset, enabling brands to command higher prices, withstand competitive pressures, and expand into new markets or product categories. Brands possessing strong brand equity enjoy a competitive edge and greater resilience in the face of market challenges.

Brand Personality

Brand personality refers to the human-like traits, characteristics, and values attributed to a brand. Consumers form judgments regarding a brand's personality based on its messaging, imagery, tone, and behavior. Brands can project personalities such as sincerity, adventure, sophistication, or innovation, resonating with diverse consumer segments and influencing their perceptions and preferences. A robust brand personality fosters emotional connections, facilitates differentiation, and guides consumer judgments and behaviors.

Brand Associations

Brand associations represent the mental connections consumers establish between a brand and specific attributes, features, or benefits. These associations may stem from product attributes (e.g., performance, design), user imagery (e.g., target demographic, lifestyle), or brand symbolism (e.g., logos, slogans). Positive associations bolster brand judgments by reinforcing desired brand attributes and forming favorable impressions in consumers' minds. Conversely, negative associations or inconsistencies between brand messaging and consumer experiences can lead to unfavorable judgments and tarnish brand perception.

Brand judgments play a pivotal role in shaping consumer perceptions, preferences, and actions. Positive assessments, such as a favorable brand perception, perceived quality, trust, loyalty, equity, personality, and associations, contribute to brand success by enhancing consumer preferences, driving purchase decisions, and fostering enduring relationships. Brands consistently delivering on promises, engaging authentically with consumers, and effectively differentiating themselves are more likely to garner positive assessments and thrive in the market. Conversely, brands failing to meet consumer expectations, betraying trust, or neglecting their brand image risk facing negative assessments that can undermine their reputation and competitive standing. Therefore, comprehending and managing brand judgments are essential for establishing and maintaining a robust brand presence and achieving sustained business success.

Case : ABC Global University

ABC is renowned for its contributions to science, technology, engineering, and mathematics (STEM) fields, and its brand is associated with innovation, cutting-edge research, and academic excellence. Stakeholders judge ABC based on various factors, including:

Perceived Quality ABC 's brand is synonymous with academic rigor, groundbreaking research, and technological innovation. Stakeholders perceive ABC as a leading institution in STEM education, shaping judgments about the quality of its programs, faculty, and facilities.

Brand Trust : ABC 's commitment to advancing knowledge, solving complex problems, and addressing global challenges builds trust among stakeholders. The institution's reputation for integrity, collaboration, and ethical conduct reinforces judgments about its reliability and credibility in the academic community.

Brand Loyalty : ABC 's brand inspires loyalty and pride among its alumni, faculty, and supporters. The perception of MIT as a trailblazer in science and technology encourages individuals to maintain strong affiliations with the institution, contribute to its success, and advocate for its continued impact.

Brand Equity : ABC 's brand equity is reflected in its global recognition, influence, and impact on innovation and entrepreneurship. The perception of ABC as a hub for creativity, problem-solving, and technological advancement enhances its brand value and distinguishes it as a leader in the competitive landscape.

Brand Personality ABC 's brand personality embodies characteristics such as curiosity, ingenuity, and ambition. The perception of MIT as a place where bold ideas are explored, and boundaries are pushed shapes judgments about its culture, values, and identity, attracting individuals who share these traits.

Brand Associations : ABC 's brand associations include symbols such as its mascot, the beaver, and iconic landmarks like the Great Dome. The perception of ABC as an emblem of scientific discovery, academic excellence, and innovation influences judgments about its brand identity and cultural significance.

ABC serves as an example of brand judgment in institutional branding, where stakeholders' perceptions, experiences, and associations with the brand shape their assessments of its quality, trustworthiness, loyalty, equity, personality, and associations. ABC 's brand image as a pioneer in science and technology reflects positive brand judgments that contribute to its esteemed reputation and impact in the academic and technological spheres. Scalability: Innovative technologies often have the potential to be scaled across different applications and markets, amplifying their impact.

11

A good reputation can't be bought; it must be earned.

Kingdom Symbolization

Symbolism of a kingdom can be a powerful metaphor in the context of institutional branding, evoking notions of strength, authority, unity, and legacy. Here's how kingdom symbolism can be applied:

Authority and Leadership

Just as a kingdom is led by a monarch, institutions can use kingdom symbolism to convey a sense of strong leadership and authority. By positioning themselves as leaders in their respective fields, institutions assert their expertise, influence, and guidance within their domain.

Unity and Community

In a kingdom, subjects are united under a common identity and purpose. Similarly, institutions can use kingdom symbolism to foster a sense of belonging and community among their members, whether they are students, faculty, staff, or alumni. By emphasizing shared values, traditions, and goals, institutions can strengthen bonds and create a cohesive community.

Legacy and Tradition

Kingdoms are often associated with rich histories, traditions, and legacies passed down through generations. Institutions can leverage kingdom symbolism to highlight their own heritage and enduring contributions to society. By showcasing milestones, achievements, and influential figures, institutions can reinforce their legacy and inspire pride among stakeholders.

Excellence and Prestige

Just as kingdoms strive for greatness and prestige, institutions can use kingdom symbolism to emphasize their pursuit of excellence and distinction. By positioning themselves as bastions of knowledge, innovation, and achievement, institutions can attract top talent, foster academic excellence, and enhance their reputation on a global scale.

Aspiration and Ambition

Kingdoms often symbolize ambition and aspiration, with rulers seeking to expand their influence and leave a lasting impact on the world. Similarly, Institutions can use kingdom symbolism to inspire ambition and drive among their members, encouraging them to pursue lofty goals and push the boundaries of knowledge and creativity.

Strength and Resilience

In the face of challenges and adversity, kingdoms demonstrate resilience and strength. Institutions can draw on kingdom symbolism to convey their ability to overcome obstacles and thrive in a competitive environment. By highlighting resilience, adaptability, and perseverance, institutions can instill confidence and trust in their ability to weather uncertainties and emerge stronger than before.

12 - L

Your brand is a reflection of your culture.

Loyalty

Institutional branding is essential for cultivating loyalty among various stakeholders, including customers, employees, students, and partners. Here's how institutional branding helps foster loyalty:

Key Components of Institutional Branding

1. Consistent Identity and Messaging

Brand Identity : Create a strong, consistent brand identity that embodies the institution's values, mission, and vision.

Visual Consistency: Maintain consistent use of logos, colors, fonts, and design elements across all platforms and materials.

2. Emotional Connection

Storytelling: : Use storytelling to create an emotional bond with your audience by sharing success stories, heritage, and impact.

Personalization: :Tailor communications to address individual needs and experiences of stakeholders.

3. Value Proposition

Unique Selling Points (USPs): : Clearly communicate what makes your institution unique. Highlight distinctive programs, services, or features.

Quality Assurance: : Ensure that the quality of your offerings consistently meets or exceeds expectations.

4. Engagement and Interaction

Community Building: Foster a sense of community through events, social media, and interactive platforms.

Feedback Mechanisms: Implement channels for feedback and show responsiveness to suggestions and concerns.

5. Trust and Credibility

Transparency: Be transparent in your operations and communications to build trust.

Accreditations and Awards Highlight any accreditations, certifications, or awards that validate your institution's credibility.

6. Employee Ambassadorship

Employee Engagement: Engage employees in the branding process and empower them to be brand ambassadors.

Training: Provide training to ensure employees understand and embody the brand values.

Strategies for Building Loyalty

Alumni Relations (for Educational Institutions)

Alumni Networks: Develop strong alumni networks that offer ongoing value through networking opportunities, events, and continuous learning.

Success Stories: Share alumni success stories to showcase the long-term benefits of association with the institution.

Customer Loyalty Programs

Rewards and Recognition: : Implement loyalty programs that reward repeat engagement or long-term association.

Exclusive Offers: Provide exclusive offers or early access to new services for loyal customers.

Corporate Social Responsibility (CSR)

Community Involvement: Engage in CSR activities that align with your brand values to enhance reputation and build goodwill.

Sustainability Initiatives: Promote and participate in sustainability initiatives that resonate with stakeholders' values.

Communication Strategy

Regular Updates: Keep stakeholders informed through regular updates via newsletters, social media, and other communication channels.

Crisis Management: Develop a robust crisis management strategy to maintain trust during challenging times.

Measuring Loyalty and Branding Effectiveness

1. Surveys and Feedback

Satisfaction Surveys: Conduct regular satisfaction surveys to gauge stakeholder **sentiments**.

Net Promoter Score (NPS): Use NPS to measure the likelihood of stakeholders recommending your institution to others.

2. Engagement Metrics

Social Media Engagement: Monitor likes, shares, comments, and other forms of engagement on social media.

Event Participation: Track participation and engagement levels in events and activities organized by the institution.

3. Retention Rates

Customer Retention: Measure the rate at which customers or members remain with the institution over time.

Employee Retention :Track employee turnover rates to ensure satisfaction and loyalty among employees.

Loyalty in institutional branding is built through consistent and authentic brand representation, fostering emotional connections, providing exceptional value, and maintaining open and transparent communication. By engaging all stakeholders and continuously measuring and adapting strategies, institutions can cultivate long-lasting loyalty that supports their overall success and growth.

13-M

"Brands are what people think of it."

Marketing mix

The marketing mix, often referred to as the 4 Ps (Product, Price, Place, Promotion), can be adapted for institutional branding to effectively communicate and strengthen the institution's brand. Here's how each element can be applied:

Product

For an institution, the "product" includes the services, experiences, and value propositions it offers. This can vary depending on whether the institution is an educational establishment, a nonprofit organization, a government entity, or a corporate entity.

Educational Institutions: Courses, degree programs, research opportunities, campus facilities, and extracurricular activities.

Nonprofits: Programs, services, advocacy efforts, and community outreach activities.

Corporates: Products, services, customer experiences, and corporate social responsibility initiatives.

Key Considerations:

Quality and Consistency: Ensure that all offerings are of high quality and consistent with the institution's values and mission.

Innovation: Continuously innovate and improve offerings to meet the evolving needs and expectations of stakeholders.

Customization: Provide personalized experiences to cater to

diverse audience segments.

Price

While institutions may not always operate with a traditional pricing model, understanding the perceived value and cost is crucial.

Educational Institutions: Tuition fees, scholarships, and financial aid.

Nonprofits: Membership fees, donation levels, and sponsorship packages.

Corporates: Pricing strategies for products and services, as well as membership or subscription models.

Key Considerations:

Affordability: Ensure that pricing strategies reflect the value provided while being accessible to the target audience.

Value Proposition: Clearly communicate the benefits and value that justify the cost, whether it's educational outcomes, societal impact, or product quality.

Financial Assistance: Offer financial aid, scholarships, or tiered pricing to accommodate different financial capabilities.

Place

Place refers to the channels and locations where the institution's offerings are made available to stakeholders.

Educational Institutions: Campus locations, online learning platforms, and satellite campuses.

Nonprofits: Community centers, online platforms, and mobile services.

Corporates Retail locations, online stores, and distribution channels.

Key Considerations:

Accessibility: Ensure that offerings are easily accessible to the target audience, whether physically or digitally.

Convenience: Make it convenient for stakeholders to engage with the institution, such as through user-friendly online platforms or well-located physical spaces.

Distribution Channels: Utilize effective distribution channels to reach a wider audience, such as partnerships, franchises, or digital platforms.

Promotion

Promotion encompasses all activities that communicate the institution's brand and offerings to the target audience.

Educational Institutions: Advertising, open houses, campus tours, social media campaigns, and alumni testimonials.

Nonprofits: Awareness campaigns, fundraising events, social media outreach, and partnerships.

Corporates: Advertising, public relations, social media marketing, influencer partnerships, and events.

Key Considerations:

Integrated Marketing Communications: : Use a mix of traditional and digital marketing strategies to reach the audience.

Engagement: Create engaging and interactive content that resonates with the audience, such as videos, blogs, and social media posts.

Public Relations: Leverage PR to build a positive image and manage the institution's reputation.

Events and Experiences: Host events and create experiences that allow stakeholders to connect with the institution and its mission.

The marketing mix for institutional branding involves tailoring the traditional 4 Ps to align with the institution's goals and the needs of its stakeholders. By focusing on high-quality offerings (Product), ensuring value and accessibility (Price), making offerings easily accessible (Place), and effectively communicating the brand (Promotion), institutions can build a strong and loyal brand presence. This holistic approach ensures that all aspects of the institution work together to create a cohesive and compelling brand identity.

Mission statements

Mission statements are crucial for institutional branding as they succinctly convey the institution's core purpose, values, and goals. They provide a clear direction and framework for decision-making, ensuring consistency in actions and communications. A well-crafted mission statement differentiates the institution from its competitors, highlighting its unique value proposition. It inspires and motivates stakeholders, including employees, students, and partners, fostering a sense of unity and commitment. Moreover, it helps attract like-minded individuals and organizations, strengthening the institution's community and network. By aligning all branding efforts with the mission statement, institutions can build trust, credibility, and a strong, cohesive brand identity that resonates with their target audience and drives long-term loyalty and support.

14-N

A brand represents its consumers.

Networking

Networking plays a pivotal role in institutional branding by fostering relationships, enhancing visibility, and building credibility. Here's how networking can benefit institutional branding:

Benefits of Networking for Institutional Branding

Increased Visibility and Reach

Expanding Audience: Networking events, conferences, and collaborations help institutions reach a wider audience.

Social Media Presence: Engaging with influencers and other organizations on social media can amplify the institution's visibility.

Building Credibility and Trust

 Partnerships: Collaborations with reputable organizations can enhance credibility.

 Endorsements: Positive testimonials and endorsements from well-known figures or institutions can build trust.

Resource Sharing and Learning

 Best Practices: Networking allows institutions to share and learn best practices, enhancing their operations and offerings.

 Access to Resources: Partnerships can provide access to resources, funding, and expertise that may not be available internally.

Community Engagement and Support

Local Involvement: Engaging with local communities and organizations fosters goodwill and strengthens community ties.

Stakeholder Relationships: Building strong relationships with stakeholders (students, parents, alumni, donors) through events and communications reinforces loyalty.

Opportunities for Collaboration

Joint Ventures: Networking can lead to joint ventures, research partnerships, or co-hosted events that enhance the institution's profile.

Innovation: Collaborations can spur innovation through the exchange of ideas and resources.

Strategies for Effective Networking in Institutional Branding

Participate in Industry Events

Attend and host conferences, seminars, and workshops relevant to your institution's field.

Engage actively in discussions, panels, and networking sessions to make meaningful connections.

Leverage Digital Platforms

Use LinkedIn, Twitter, and other professional networks to connect with industry leaders and influencers.

Join relevant online communities and forums to engage in conversations and share insights.

Develop Strategic Partnerships

Identify and collaborate with organizations that share similar values and goals.

Create mutually beneficial partnerships that enhance both

parties' brand and reach.

Alumni Networks and Ambassadors

Engage alumni through events, newsletters, and social media to keep them connected and involved.

Empower alumni to serve as brand ambassadors, sharing their positive experiences and successes.

Local Community Involvement

Participate in or sponsor local events, charities, and community projects.

Build relationships with local businesses, government entities, and other organizations.

Measuring the Impact of Networking

Engagement Metrics

Track participation and engagement at events, both online and offline.

Monitor social media interactions, such as likes, shares, and comments.

Partnership Outcomes

Assess the success of collaborations and partnerships through joint projects and initiatives.

Measure the impact of resource sharing and best practice exchanges.

Brand Awareness and Perception

Conduct surveys and gather feedback to understand how networking efforts have influenced brand perception.

Use analytics to measure changes in website traffic, social media reach, and other visibility indicators.

Networking is a powerful tool for institutional branding, enhancing visibility, credibility, and community engagement. By strategically participating in industry events, leveraging digital platforms, forming partnerships, engaging alumni, and involving the local community, institutions can build strong networks that support and strengthen their brand. Measuring the impact of these efforts ensures continuous improvement and sustained success.

15-O

Brand is one of the Assets of the Company.

OMG

Creating an "Oh My God" (OMG) feeling for institutional branding involves delivering experiences and messages that evoke strong, positive emotional reactions. This emotional connection can transform stakeholders into passionate advocates and loyal supporters. Here's how to achieve this:

Strategies for Creating an OMG Feeling in Institutional Branding

Exceptional Experiences

Surprise and Delight: Go beyond expectations in every interaction, whether it's through exceptional customer service, unique campus experiences, or special events.

Innovative Offerings: Introduce innovative programs, services, or facilities that stand out and make a lasting impression.

Powerful Storytelling

Compelling Narratives: Share inspiring stories of success, impact, and transformation that resonate emotionally with your audience.

Authenticity: Ensure that stories are genuine and align with the institution's core values and mission.

Engaging Visuals and Media

High-Quality Visuals: Use stunning photography, videography, and graphic design to capture attention and evoke emotion.

Virtual Reality (VR) and Augmented Reality (AR): - Implement VR and AR experiences to provide immersive and memorable engagements.

Personalization

Tailored Communication: Customize interactions and communications to make stakeholders feel valued and understood.

Unique Journeys: Offer personalized experiences and pathways that cater to individual needs and preferences.

Exceptional Facilities and Environment

Awe-Inspiring Spaces: Design and maintain beautiful, inspiring physical spaces that leave a lasting impression.

Cutting-Edge Technology: Integrate advanced technology to enhance the user experience and demonstrate innovation.

Exclusive Opportunities

VIP Experiences: Create exclusive events, access, or programs that make stakeholders feel special and privileged.

Behind-the-Scenes Access: Offer behind-the-scenes tours or insights that provide a unique perspective and deeper connection.

Emotional Engagement

Empathy and Care: Show genuine care and empathy in all interactions, making stakeholders feel valued and respected.

Celebration of Milestones: Celebrate achievements, anniversaries, and milestones with stakeholders to build a shared sense of pride.

Community and Belonging

Inclusive Culture: Foster an inclusive and welcoming culture that makes everyone feel part of a larger family.

Active Engagement: Engage stakeholders in meaningful ways, encouraging participation and involvement in the institution's activities.

Examples of OMG Branding Tactics

Surprise Gifts or Tokens: Sending unexpected gifts or tokens of appreciation to students, alumni, or partners.

High-Profile Speakers or Events: Hosting renowned speakers, celebrities, or extraordinary events that leave a memorable impact.

Innovative Campaigns: Launching creative and unexpected marketing campaigns that go viral and generate buzz.

Memorable Campus Tours: Offering immersive and unique

campus tours that showcase the institution's best features in an unforgettable way.

Success Stories and Testimonials: Sharing powerful testimonials and stories of remarkable achievements from students, faculty, and alumni.

Measuring the Impact

Emotional Response Surveys: Collect feedback on how stakeholders feel about their experiences and interactions with the institution.

Engagement Metrics: Monitor engagement levels on social media, event participation, and other interactive platforms.

Brand Perception Studies: Conduct studies to assess changes in brand perception and emotional connection over time.

Referral and Advocacy Rates: Track referral rates and the number of stakeholders actively promoting the institution.

Creating an OMG feeling for institutional branding requires a strategic focus on delivering exceptional, emotionally resonant experiences that exceed expectations. By prioritizing surprise and delight, powerful storytelling, engaging visuals, personalization, and community building, institutions can forge deep emotional connections that inspire loyalty and advocacy. Continuously measuring and adapting these efforts ensures sustained impact and a strong, memorable brand.

16-P

Business is not a commodity it is a Brand.

PR

Partnerships strategic

Strategic partnerships can significantly enhance institutional branding by leveraging the strengths, resources, and networks of partner organizations. These collaborations can boost visibility, credibility, and impact, creating a more compelling brand presence. Here's how to approach strategic partnerships for institutional branding:

Benefits of Strategic Partnerships

Expanded Reach and Visibility

Partnering with well-known organizations can help extend your institution's reach to new audiences and markets.

Joint events, campaigns, and initiatives increase exposure across multiple platforms.

Enhanced Credibility and Trust

Associations with reputable partners enhance the institution's credibility.

Collaborative endorsements can build trust among stakehold

Resource Sharing and Innovation**

Sharing resources such as expertise, technology, and funding can lead to innovative projects and initiatives.

Joint research, development, and educational programs can enhance the institution's offerings.

Community Engagement and Support

Partnerships with community organizations can strengthen local ties and improve community relations.

Engaging in joint community service projects can demonstrate the institution's commitment to social responsibility.

Mutual Learning and Growth

Collaborating with other institutions or organizations provides opportunities for mutual learning and growth.

Best practice exchanges can improve operational efficiencies and outcomes.

Strategies for Developing Strategic Partnerships

Identify Potential Partners

Alignment of Values: Look for organizations with similar values, mission, and goals.

Complementary Strengths: Identify partners whose strengths complement your institution's weaknesses or gaps.

Define Clear Objectives

Establish clear, mutually beneficial goals for the partnership.

Outline specific outcomes, such as increased enrollment, enhanced research capabilities, or community impact.

Develop Collaborative Programs

Create joint programs, such as dual-degree offerings, research projects, or community initiatives.

Host co-branded events, workshops, and conferences to showcase the partnership.

Formalize the Partnership

Develop a formal agreement or Memorandum of Understanding (MOU) to outline roles, responsibilities, and expectations.

Establish governance structures and regular communication channels to manage the partnership.

Promote the Partnership

Use joint marketing and PR efforts to promote the partnership and its initiatives.

Share success stories and outcomes through various media channels to highlight the impact of the collaboration.

Examples of Effective Strategic Partnerships

Educational Collaborations

Universities partnering with tech companies to offer specialized training and certification programs.

Joint research initiatives between academic institutions and industry leaders.

Corporate Partnerships

Companies sponsoring educational programs or providing internships and career opportunities for students.

Collaboration on CSR initiatives, such as sustainability projects or community development programs.

Nonprofit and Government Alliances

Institutions working with nonprofits to address social issues, such as poverty, education, and health.

Partnerships with government agencies to support policy development and public service projects.

Measuring the Impact

Key Performance Indicators (KPIs)

- Track metrics such as enrollment numbers, research output, community engagement levels, and media coverage.

Measure the return on investment (ROI) in terms of financial gains, resource savings, and impact on brand perception.

Stakeholder Feedback

Collect feedback from students, faculty, partners, and the community to assess the effectiveness and satisfaction with the partnership.

Use surveys, focus groups, and interviews to gather insights and identify areas for improvement.

Regular Reviews and Adjustments

- Conduct regular reviews of the partnership's progress and outcomes.

- Adjust strategies and goals as needed to ensure continued alignment and mutual benefit.

Strategic partnerships are a powerful tool for enhancing institutional branding. By collaborating with aligned organizations, institutions can expand their reach, enhance credibility, and innovate more effectively. Clear objectives, formal agreements, and proactive promotion are key to successful partnerships. Regular measurement and adjustment ensure these collaborations continue to deliver value and strengthen the institution's brand over time.

17-Q

The experiences of the customers, people, organizations is

Brand.

Quality Assurance

Quality assurance is crucial for institutional branding as it ensures that all aspects of the institution's offerings and communications consistently meet high standards. This consistency helps build trust, credibility, and a strong reputation. Here's how to implement quality assurance for institutional branding:

Key Elements of Quality Assurance for Institutional Branding

Consistent Brand Messaging

Brand Guidelines: Develop comprehensive brand guidelines that outline the proper use of logos, colors, fonts, tone, and messaging.

Training: Provide regular training for employees to ensure they understand and adhere to brand standards.

High-Quality Offerings

Programs and Services: Ensure that all programs, courses, and services meet high standards of quality and relevance.

Continuous Improvement: Regularly review and update offerings based on feedback, industry trends, and new research.

Stakeholder Feedback

Surveys and Feedback Forms: Collect regular feedback from students, faculty, alumni, and other stakeholders to gauge satisfaction and identify areas for improvement.

Focus Groups: Conduct focus groups to gain deeper insights into stakeholder perceptions and experiences.

Performance Metrics

KPIs: Establish key performance indicators (KPIs) to measure the effectiveness of branding efforts, such as enrollment rates, retention rates, and social media engagement.

 Benchmarking: Compare performance against industry standards and competitors to identify strengths and areas for improvement.

Accreditations and Certifications

Accreditation Bodies: Seek accreditations from recognized bodies to validate the quality of your programs and operations.

Certifications: Obtain relevant certifications to demonstrate compliance with industry standards and best practices.

Quality Control Processes

Regular Audits: Conduct regular audits of marketing materials, website content, and other communications to ensure consistency and accuracy.

Standard Operating Procedures (SOPs): Develop and implement SOPs for creating and reviewing branded content.

Employee Engagement and Training

Onboarding Programs: Include brand training in onboarding

programs for new employees to ensure they understand the institution's values and standards.

Professional Development: Offer ongoing professional development opportunities to keep staff updated on best practices and new developments in branding and quality assurance.

Technology and Tools

Content Management Systems (CMS): Use CMS to ensure consistency and quality of online content.

Analytics Tools: Utilize analytics tools to monitor and evaluate the effectiveness of branding initiatives.

Strategies for Implementing Quality Assurance

Develop a Quality Assurance Framework

Define Standards: Clearly define the quality standards for all aspects of the institution's offerings and communications.

Assign Responsibilities: Designate roles and responsibilities for quality assurance tasks to ensure accountability.

Engage Stakeholders

Feedback Loops: Create feedback loops to continuously gather and act on stakeholder input.

Transparency: Communicate quality assurance processes and improvements to stakeholders to build trust and engagement.

Regular Reviews and Updates

Periodic Assessments: Conduct periodic assessments of branding materials and strategies to ensure they remain effective and relevant.

Continuous Improvement: Implement a continuous improvement cycle based on feedback and performance data.

Measuring Quality Assurance Impact

Stakeholder Satisfaction

 Survey Results: Analyze survey results to measure satisfaction levels and identify trends over time.

 Net Promoter Score (NPS): Use NPS to gauge stakeholder loyalty and likelihood to recommend the institution.

Performance Data

Enrollment and Retention Rates: Monitor these rates to assess the impact of branding on attracting and retaining students.

Engagement Metrics: Track engagement metrics across digital and physical platforms to measure the reach and impact of branding efforts.

Accreditation and Certification Outcomes

 Accreditation Reports: Review accreditation reports for insights into areas of excellence and areas needing improvement.

Certification Status: Monitor the status of certifications to ensure ongoing compliance and quality.

Quality assurance in institutional branding is about maintaining high standards and consistency across all interactions and communications. By developing robust quality assurance processes, engaging stakeholders, and continuously monitoring and improving efforts, institutions can build a strong, trustworthy brand that stands out in a competitive landscape. This leads to enhanced credibility, stakeholder satisfaction, and long-term success.

18-R

A brand is an idea inside the prospects.

Research Methods

Reputation Management

Research methods are vital for institutional branding as they provide the necessary insights and data to shape, refine, and evaluate branding strategies effectively. These methods ensure that branding efforts resonate with stakeholders, remain competitive, and align with the institution's goals and values.

Understanding Stakeholders

Firstly, research methods such as surveys, interviews, and focus groups help institutions understand their stakeholders' perceptions, needs, and expectations. This understanding is crucial for creating a brand that resonates with current and prospective students, alumni, faculty, and the broader community. Knowing what stakeholders value and how they perceive the institution allows for tailored messaging and offerings that strengthen emotional connections and loyalty.

Competitive Positioning

Secondly, competitive analysis enables institutions to identify their unique selling points and differentiate themselves in the market. By analyzing competitors' branding strategies, strengths, and weaknesses, institutions can carve out a distinct niche, emphasize their unique qualities, and avoid potential pitfalls. This strategic differentiation is essential for attracting and retaining stakeholders in a crowded educational landscape.

Data-Driven Decision Making

Thirdly, the use of quantitative methods like surveys and social media analytics provides data-driven insights that inform branding decisions. These methods offer measurable metrics on brand awareness, stakeholder satisfaction, and engagement levels, which are critical for evaluating the effectiveness of branding campaigns and initiatives. Continuous monitoring through these methods ensures that branding efforts are adaptable and responsive to changing trends and stakeholder feedback.

Enhancing Credibility and Trust

Additionally, brand audits and ethnographic research contribute to maintaining consistency and authenticity in branding. Regular audits ensure that all branding materials and communications align with the institution's core values and messaging, reinforcing credibility and trust among stakeholders. Ethnographic research offers deep contextual insights, helping institutions create more authentic and meaningful brand experiences.

Continuous Improvement

Finally, secondary data analysis and case studies provide valuable lessons from past branding efforts, both successful and unsuccessful. Learning from these experiences allows institutions to continuously improve their branding strategies, innovate, and stay ahead of the curve.

Research methods are indispensable for institutional branding. They enable a comprehensive understanding of stakeholders, inform competitive positioning, support data-driven decision-making, enhance credibility, and facilitate continuous improvement. By leveraging these methods, institutions can build strong, effective, and enduring brands that resonate deeply with their audiences.

Reputation Management

Reputation management holds critical importance in institutional branding strategies, directly influencing stakeholder perceptions and engagement. Its significance lies in nurturing trust, credibility, and loyalty among stakeholders such as students, alumni, faculty, and the wider community. A positive reputation not only sets the institution apart from competitors but also attracts top talent and fosters valuable partnerships and funding opportunities.

Strategies for effective reputation management entail ensuring consistent alignment between branding messages and institutional actions to maintain authenticity and trustworthiness. Open and transparent communication is pivotal, addressing concerns openly and honestly to foster trust. Upholding high standards of quality across all aspects of operations is essential, reinforcing a positive reputation.

Vigilant monitoring of both online and offline channels for feedback and mentions allows for prompt responses to any issues or negative sentiments, minimizing reputational damage. Additionally, engaging stakeholders regularly and involving them in decision-making processes fosters a sense of ownership and loyalty. By prioritizing reputation management within branding strategies, institutions can cultivate a positive image, enhance trust, and secure their long-term success in a competitive environment.

19-S

Marketing makes the Brand through its processes.

Social Media

Stakeholder Engagement

Storytelling

Social media strategies are pivotal for institutional branding, offering a dynamic platform to engage stakeholders, exhibit institutional values, and extend brand reach. Here's how to effectively utilize social media for institutional branding:

Tailored Content Creation: Customize content to resonate with diverse audience segments, including prospective students, alumni, faculty, and the wider community. Share compelling narratives, achievements, and updates that underscore the institution's mission and influence.

Unified Branding Maintain consistent brand identity across all social media channels, encompassing visual elements, tone, and messaging. This consistency reinforces brand recognition and authenticity.

Active Engagement: Proactively interact with followers by promptly responding to comments, messages, and tags. Foster dialogue, pose questions, and solicit feedback to cultivate a sense of community and involvement.

Visual Storytelling: Harness the power of visual content such as photos, videos, and infographics to convey key messages and showcase the institution's ethos, culture, and milestones effectively.

Strategic Platform Selection: Opt for social media platforms that align with institutional objectives and target audience demographics. Focus efforts on platforms where engagement and visibility can be maximized.

Data-driven Optimization: Regularly analyze social media metrics to assess performance, detect trends, and refine content strategies. Adapt approaches based on insights to ensure continual enhancement and efficacy.

By implementing these social media tactics, institutions can fortify their brand presence, cultivate meaningful connections with stakeholders, and bolster their standing and impact in the digital sphere.

Stakeholder Engagement

Stakeholder engagement is vital for institutional branding as it fosters a sense of community, builds trust, and enhances brand loyalty. By involving stakeholders such as students, alumni, faculty, staff, and the wider community in branding initiatives, institutions can create a shared sense of ownership and pride in the institution's identity and achievements. This can be achieved through various channels such as events, surveys, focus groups, and social media interactions. Actively seeking and incorporating stakeholder feedback ensures that branding efforts resonate authentically and effectively with the target audience. Moreover, engaging stakeholders in decision-making processes and showcasing their contributions reinforces their connection to the institution, ultimately strengthening the brand's reputation and influence.

Storytelling

Storytelling is a powerful strategy for institutional branding, allowing institutions to convey their mission, values, and impact in a compelling and relatable way. Here are key storytelling strategies:

Highlighting Personal Narratives: Share stories of individuals within the institution—students, faculty, alumni, and community members—to humanize the brand and illustrate its impact on real lives.

Showcasing Achievements and Milestones: Use storytelling to celebrate successes, milestones, and achievements, demonstrating the institution's dedication to excellence and innovation.

Creating Emotional Connections: Craft narratives that evoke emotion and resonate with stakeholders, inspiring pride, empathy, or aspiration.

Consistency Across Platforms: Ensure storytelling is consistent across all communication channels, including website content, social media posts, videos, and print materials, reinforcing the institution's brand identity and messaging.

Authenticity and Transparency: Be authentic and transparent in storytelling, sharing both successes and challenges to build trust and credibility with stakeholders.

20-T

Choose media so useful people would pay you for it

Target demographics

Traditional Media

Identifying target demographics is crucial for effective institutional branding. By understanding the characteristics, preferences, and needs of specific audience segments, institutions can tailor their branding strategies to resonate more deeply and engage more effectively with their intended audience.

One primary demographic for institutional branding is prospective students. This includes high school students exploring higher education options, transfer students considering a change, and adult learners seeking career advancement or personal enrichment. Understanding their academic interests, career goals, and lifestyle preferences allows institutions to showcase relevant programs, facilities, and opportunities that align with their aspirations.

Another key demographic is alumni, who play a significant role in shaping the institution's reputation and future success. Alumni branding efforts aim to foster lifelong connections, pride, and support among graduates. By highlighting alumni achievements, providing networking opportunities, and offering continued educational and social experiences, institutions can maintain strong ties with this valuable demographic.

Faculty and staff also represent important stakeholders in institutional branding. Recognizing their contributions, expertise, and professional development needs is essential for fostering a positive institutional culture and attracting top talent. Branding efforts targeting faculty and staff may focus on highlighting research opportunities, professional development programs, and benefits that contribute to their success and satisfaction.

Lastly, the broader community, including local residents, businesses, and organizations, forms an integral part of an institution's brand ecosystem. Engaging with the community through partnerships, outreach programs, and cultural events not only enhances the institution's visibility and reputation but also demonstrates its commitment to social responsibility and civic engagement.

Understanding and effectively targeting key demographics such as prospective students, alumni, faculty and staff, and the broader community are essential for successful institutional branding. By tailoring branding strategies to meet the specific needs and interests of each demographic, institutions can build stronger connections, enhance reputation, and drive long-term success.

Traditional Media

Traditional media remains a significant channel for institutional branding, offering broad reach and credibility. Here's how institutions leverage traditional media:

Print Publications: Institutions often feature in newspapers, magazines, and newsletters to share news, achievements, and thought leadership articles. Print publications lend credibility and authority to the institution's messaging, reaching a diverse audience including alumni, donors, and local communities.

Broadcast Media: Television and radio appearances provide opportunities for institutions to showcase their expertise, research, and initiatives. Interviews, panel discussions, and sponsored segments allow institutions to reach a wide audience and position themselves as leaders in their field.

Outdoor Advertising: Billboards, banners, and signage in strategic locations can increase brand visibility and awareness within the local community. Outdoor advertising is particularly effective for promoting events, campus tours, and enrollment periods.

Direct Mail: Sending physical mailers, brochures, and newsletters to targeted audiences, such as prospective students or alumni, can generate interest and engagement. Direct mail campaigns can be personalized and tailored to specific demographics, increasing their effectiveness.

Events and Sponsorships: Participating in or sponsoring community events, conferences, and industry exhibitions provides opportunities for institutions to connect with stakeholders in person. Public speaking engagements and hosting informational sessions can further enhance brand visibility and credibility.

Despite the rise of digital media, traditional media channels continue to play a vital role in institutional branding by complementing online efforts and reaching audiences who may not be as active online. By strategically leveraging traditional media, institutions can effectively enhance their brand presence, engage stakeholders, and achieve their branding objectives.

A brand has feelings of customers.

Umbrella Brand

An umbrella brand serves as an overarching identity that encompasses multiple entities or offerings within an institution. Here's how an umbrella brand can benefit institutional branding:

Consistency and Cohesion: An umbrella brand provides consistency across various departments, programs, and initiatives within the institution. This cohesive identity strengthens brand recognition and reinforces the institution's values and mission.

Streamlined Communication: By centralizing branding efforts under one umbrella, institutions can streamline communication and messaging. This clarity ensures that stakeholders understand the interconnectedness of different entities and fosters a unified

perception of the institution.

Cost Efficiency: Developing and promoting a single umbrella

brand can be more cost-effective than managing multiple

independent brands. It reduces the need for separate marketing

campaigns and allows for shared resources and infrastructure.

Risk Management: An umbrella brand can help mitigate risks

associated with individual brands. If one entity faces a

reputational issue, the strength of the umbrella brand can help

protect the overall institution's reputation.

Flexibility and Scalability: As institutions evolve and expand, an

umbrella brand provides flexibility to accommodate new entities,

programs, or initiatives. This scalability allows for organic growth while maintaining a coherent brand identity.

Overall, an umbrella brand offers numerous advantages for institutional branding, including consistency, streamlined communication, cost efficiency, risk management, and scalability. By effectively leveraging an umbrella brand, institutions can enhance their brand presence, strengthen stakeholder relationships, and achieve their branding objectives more effectively.

22-V

People buy what they believe is right.

Visual identity

Vision statement

Visual identity is a cornerstone of institutional branding, encompassing the visual elements that represent the institution's personality, values, and mission. This includes the logo, color palette, typography, imagery, and graphic elements used across various communication channels. A strong visual identity creates consistency and cohesion, reinforcing brand recognition and credibility among stakeholders. The logo serves as the centerpiece, embodying the essence of the institution and providing a recognizable symbol that is instantly associated with its brand. The color palette communicates emotions, themes, and brand attributes, while typography establishes a consistent tone and personality. Imagery and graphic elements further enhance the visual identity, conveying the institution's culture, diversity, and achievements. By carefully crafting and maintaining a cohesive visual identity, institutions can effectively communicate their brand story, establish a strong brand presence, and foster meaningful connections with their audience.

Vision statement

Aligning the vision statement with institutional branding is pivotal for establishing a cohesive and influential brand identity. A vision statement encapsulates the institution's long-term aspirations and values, serving as a guiding beacon for all branding endeavors. When seamlessly integrated into branding strategies, it provides a clear direction, ensuring that every communication and visual element reflects the institution's overarching goals and beliefs. This alignment fosters authenticity and consistency, reinforcing the institution's identity and reputation across various platforms and touchpoints. Moreover, a compelling vision statement inspires stakeholders, instilling a sense of purpose and

commitment among students, faculty, staff, alumni, and donors.

By aligning branding efforts with the institution's vision, it not

only cultivates loyalty and support but also distinguishes the

institution in a competitive landscape, attracting individuals who

resonate with its values and aspirations. Ultimately, this

alignment lays the foundation for long-term success, enabling the

institution to build a strong, enduring brand that reflects its

unique identity and leaves a lasting impact on its stakeholders and

community.

23-W

All of us need to understand the importance of branding.

website branding

A website serves as a central hub for institutional branding, offering a digital platform to convey the institution's identity, values, and offerings. An effective website branding strategy begins with a cohesive visual identity, incorporating elements such as the logo, color palette, typography, and imagery to create a consistent and memorable brand experience. Through strategic design and layout, the website should reflect the institution's personality and culture, providing visitors with a compelling and immersive journey. Clear navigation and intuitive user experience ensure that stakeholders can easily access relevant information, whether they are prospective students exploring academic programs, alumni seeking updates on campus events, or donors looking to support initiatives. Moreover, engaging content, such as success stories, faculty profiles, and interactive multimedia, brings the institution's brand to life, showcasing its impact and achievements. By leveraging the website as a powerful branding tool, institutions can effectively communicate their unique value proposition, strengthen stakeholder relationships, and elevate their brand presence in the digital landscape.

Website branding for institutional branding involves several key strategies to effectively convey the institution's identity and engage visitors:

Cohesive Visual Identity: Ensure that the website design aligns with the institution's visual identity, including the logo, color scheme, typography, and imagery. Consistency in these elements reinforces brand recognition and professionalism.

User-Centric Design: Prioritize user experience (UX) and user interface (UI) design to create a seamless and intuitive browsing experience. Clear navigation, logical layout, and mobile responsiveness enhance usability and encourage exploration.

Compelling Content: Develop engaging and informative content that highlights the institution's unique value proposition, academic programs, faculty expertise, student achievements, and campus life. Incorporate multimedia elements, such as videos, photos, and infographics, to make the content visually appealing and interactive.

Storytelling: Use storytelling techniques to convey the institution's history, mission, values, and impact. Personal narratives, success stories, and testimonials humanize the brand and create emotional connections with visitors.

Call-to-Action (CTA) Placement: Strategically place CTAs throughout the website to encourage desired actions, such as scheduling a campus tour, applying for admission, donating to the institution, or subscribing to newsletters. Clear and compelling CTAs guide visitors through the conversion funnel.

Accessibility: Ensure that the website is accessible to all users, including those with disabilities. Adhere to web accessibility standards (e.g., WCAG) to provide an inclusive experience for everyone.

Search Engine Optimization (SEO): Optimize website content and structure for search engines to improve visibility and attract organic traffic. Use relevant keywords, meta tags, and descriptive URLs to enhance search engine rankings.

Analytics and Optimization: Implement web analytics tools (e.g., Google Analytics) to track user behavior, engagement metrics, and conversion rates. Use data insights to continuously optimize website performance and user experience.

By implementing these strategies, institutions can create a website that effectively communicates their brand identity, engages visitors, and drives desired actions, ultimately contributing to the institution's overall branding and success.

24-X

Branding demands commitment to follow emotions of the customers.

Xquisite

Xquisite - Brand Excellence Achievement signifies the pinnacle of institutional branding, embodying a commitment to unparalleled quality, innovation, and impact. This achievement is attained through a strategic blend of meticulous branding initiatives that elevate the institution's reputation, foster stakeholder trust, and set new standards of excellence in the industry. It encompasses a comprehensive approach to branding that prioritizes authenticity, creativity, and relevance, ensuring that every aspect of the institution's identity resonates deeply with its audience. From visionary leadership and cohesive visual identity to compelling

storytelling and exceptional user experience, every facet of the

institution's brand reflects a dedication to excellence and a

relentless pursuit of greatness. The Xquisite Brand Excellence

Achievement not only distinguishes the institution as a leader in

its field but also inspires admiration, loyalty, and admiration

among stakeholders, cementing its legacy as a beacon of

excellence in the educational landscape.

Achieving "Xquisite Brand Excellence" for institutional branding

requires a multifaceted approach. Key strategies include

meticulous market research to understand audience perceptions

and needs, crafting a compelling brand narrative that resonates

emotionally with stakeholders, and developing a cohesive visual

identity that reinforces the brand's values and differentiation.

Consistent communication across all channels, both traditional

and digital, helps amplify the brand message and engage with

diverse audiences. Building strong partnerships and collaborations

further enhances brand visibility and credibility. Continuous monitoring and adaptation based on feedback and performance metrics ensure the brand remains relevant and impactful. Ultimately, investing in these strategies fosters long-term brand loyalty, trust, and recognition, establishing the institution as a leader in its field and exemplifying excellence in every aspect of its branding efforts.

25-Y

The values of the company portrays its brand.

Yearly Budget

Determining a yearly budget for institutional branding depends on various factors, including the institution's size, goals, target audience, and existing brand presence. However, a general guideline is to allocate around 5% to 10% of the institution's overall budget to branding activities. For example, a larger institution with a significant focus on branding and marketing might allocate closer to 10% of its budget, while a smaller institution may allocate around 5%.

Within this budget, expenses may include:

Brand Development: Costs associated with developing or refreshing the institution's brand identity, including logo design, brand guidelines, and visual assets.

Marketing Collateral   Printing costs for brochures, flyers, posters, and other promotional materials, as well as design fees.

Digital Marketing: Expenses related to online advertising, social media marketing, search engine optimization (SEO), and email marketing campaigns.

Website Maintenance: Costs for website hosting, domain registration, content management system (CMS) updates, and ongoing website development.

Events and Sponsorships: Funding for hosting or participating in events, conferences, and sponsorships to promote the

institution's brand.

Public Relations: Fees for media relations, press releases, and PR

campaigns to enhance the institution's visibility and reputation.

Market Research: Budget for conducting market research,

surveys, focus groups, and other methods to gather insights into

audience preferences and perceptions.

Staffing: Salaries and benefits for marketing and branding

personnel, as well as training and professional development

expenses.

It's essential to regularly review and adjust the branding budget

based on performance metrics, evolving goals, and changes in the competitive landscape to ensure optimal allocation of resources

and maximum return on investment.

26-Z

A premium brand has a better delivery in terms of quality and ease to customers.

Zeal

Zeal for Institutional Branding encapsulates a fervent dedication and enthusiasm towards crafting and enhancing the identity, reputation, and impact of an institution. It signifies a proactive and passionate approach to branding that goes beyond mere marketing tactics, reflecting a deep commitment to aligning the institution's values, mission, and aspirations with its external image and perception. This zeal drives stakeholders to continuously innovate, differentiate, and elevate the institution's brand presence, leveraging creativity, authenticity, and strategic thinking to captivate audiences and foster meaningful connections. It inspires a culture of excellence, collaboration, and continuous improvement, where every branding initiative is infused with energy, purpose, and a relentless pursuit of excellence. Ultimately, the Zeal for Institutional Branding ignites a sense of pride, loyalty, and admiration among stakeholders, propelling the institution towards greater recognition, influence, and success in the competitive landscape.

Ultimate Conclusion

There are recommended approaches for how institutions, communities, and families can collaborate to create strong partnerships, makng the institution a supportive environment, second only to home. These approaches focus on strategies to overcome common challenges to community involvement in the institution. Key strategies include:

1. Overcoming limitations of time and resources.

2. Providing information and training for both parents and staff.

3. Restructuring the institution to better support community involvement.

4. Bridging differences between the institution and communities.

5. Leveraging external resources to strengthen partnerships.

While in educational institutions, recruiters are among the most important stakeholders. Ultimately, they represent the students' destination after graduation, where the training and knowledge acquired are put to the test in real-world performance. A recruiter's repeated engagement with an institution is directly tied to their satisfaction with the students' preparedness and skills imparted by the institution. This study highlights the importance of providing quality infrastructure and amenities, as they play a significant role in brand building and contribute to the long-term sustainability of an educational institution.

Bibliography

1. *Keller, Kevin Lane (1998), Strategic Brand Management: Building, Measuring and Managing Brand Equity. Upper Saddle River, NJ: Prentice-Hall.(p172)*

2. *Philip Kotler & Waldemar Pfoertsch, "Ingredient Branding- Making the Invisible Visible", Springer-2010. (p.192-196)*

3. *S.A. Chunawala, "Compendium of Brand Management", Himalaya Publishing house-2011.(p. 143)*

4. *IICMR Journal, ISSN NO. 0975-2757, Vol 4 March-2010.(p.26)*

5. *Indian Journal of Marketing, ISSN 0973-8703, June-2013 (p.27)*

6. *Marketing Communication Strategy, ICMR June, 2000. (p.28)*

7. *Business Today, October 3, 2010. (p.15-17)*

8. *Business India, B-Schools Directory 2011. (p.111-129)*

9. *Asker.D.A. (1991), "Managing Brand Equity, "New York, N.Y. Freee Press p. 17*

10. *Bagozzi, R.P. & Yi, Y (1998), "The Evaluation of Structural Equation Models" Journal of the Academy of Marketing Science,16 (1) p74-94*

11. *Branding 2014 February 8:*

   http://mktsci.journal.informs.org/content/25/6/740.short

12. *Brand Building 2014 February 9: http://www.consulted.biz*

13. Hatch, M. J. (2017). The dynamics of organizational identity. Routledge.

14. Schultz, M., Hatch, M. J., & Larsen, M. H. (2000). The expressive organization: Linking identity, reputation, and the corporate brand. Oxford University Press.

15. Aaker, D. A. (1991). Managing brand equity: Capitalizing on the value of a brand name. Free Press.

16. de Chernatony, L. (2010). From brand vision to brand evaluation: The strategic process of growing and strengthening brands. Routledge.

17. Fombrun, C. J., & Van Riel, C. B. (2004). Fame & fortune: How successful companies build winning reputations. Financial Times Prentice Hall.

18. Keller, K. L., & Lehmann, D. R. (2006). Brands and branding: Research findings and future priorities. Marketing Science, 25(6), 740-759.

19. Olins, W. (2003). On brand. Thames & Hudson.

20. Ind, N., & Coote, L. (2004). Branding and advertising. SAGE Publications.

21. Kapferer, J. N. (2004). The new strategic brand management: Creating and sustaining brand equity long term. Kogan Page Publishers.

22. Aaker, D. A., & Joachimsthaler, E. (2000). Brand leadership. Simon and Schuster.

23. Aaker, D. A. (1996). Building strong brands. Simon and Schuster.

24. Hatch, M. J., & Schultz, M. (2010). Toward a theory of brand co-creation with implications for brand governance. Journal of Brand Management, 17(8), 590-604.

25. Keller, K. L. (1993). Conceptualizing, measuring, and managing customer-based brand equity. Journal of Marketing, 57(1), 1-22.

26. Kotler, P., & Keller, K. L. (2016). Marketing management. Pearson.

27. Kapferer, J. N. (2012). The new strategic brand management: Advanced insights and strategic thinking. Kogan Page Publishers.

28. Balmer, J. M. T., & Greyser, S. A. (2003). Revealing the corporation: Perspectives on identity, image, reputation, corporate branding, and corporate-level marketing. Routledge.

29. Davis, D., & Dunn, M. (2002). Building a successful brand: Branding basics. Journal of Business Strategy, 23(4), 26-31.

30. Fombrun, C. J. (1996). Reputation: Realizing value from the corporate image. Harvard Business Press.

&

Times of India

Economic Times

The Hindu

The New York Times

The Financial Times

HBR (Harvard Business Review)

ABOUT THE AUTHOR

Dr. Shyam Shukla is presently a BusinessProfessor at NSB, Bangalore. Prior to this, he had taught at Linnaeus University, Sweden. He held the position of Senior Faculty at Bharati Vidyapeeth (Deemed to be University) Institute of Management and Entrepreneurship Development, Pune.

He has also served as the Dean – Industry Institute Interaction, and as the former Director and Principal In-Charge of the Central Institute of Business Management Research & Development, Nagpur.

Dr. Shukla has been the Executive Chairman of the International Centre for Spiritualism and Leadership. He was the founding member and former President of the National Human Resource Development Network, Nagpur Chapter. He is also a member of the Decision Sciences Institute, USA, and served as the Chairman for the Nagpur Region of the Association of Management of MBA/MMS Institutes (AMMI), Pune.

He holds a Master's degree and a Ph.D. in Business Administration. Dr. Shukla has further specialized in the areas of International Business, Environmental Engineering, and Public Relations.

An accomplished author, Dr. Shukla has written many books focusing on International Business and Research Methodology. Professionally, he has contributed to numerous organizations across India including Golf Course Delhi, Birla Global Asset Fin Co. Ltd., Professional C&F, and Ashok Leyland, among others.

Dr. Shukla has provided consultancy services and training programs to various organizations. He has conducted numerous workshops and seminars, particularly in the fields of Human Resource Development (HRD) and Women Empowerment.

A firm believer in youth empowerment, Dr. Shukla emphasizes equipping students with global perspectives and knowledge in Foreign Trade. He is also well-versed in Psychometric Testing, Neuro-Linguistic Programming (NLP), and Transactional Analysis.

In his leisure time, Dr. Shukla enjoys mentoring, networking, photography, and traveling.